"This book tells an a[...] resilience, and love throu[...] precisely what we need to help us understand the struggles and joys of disabled children and their families. Barbara's ability to reflect honestly on her journey is a wonderful resource and inspiration. From the minute I started reading this book, I couldn't put it down."

—ROULA ALKHOURI
Associate Pastor for Children and Youth
First Presbyterian Church, Bend, Oregon

How the Lilies Grow is the gripping story of a remarkable woman's struggle to meet the needs of her developmentally disabled daughter. It reveals the insensitive reactions of a culture that worships beauty and intelligence and the impersonal and sometimes violent treatment afforded the disabled in institutions and by 'professionals.' Yet it also reveals the heartbreaking grace in the help of both friends and strangers and the author's personal growth that occurred during her struggle. If you read this book, you'll never again take for granted the gift of your 'normal' child—or close your heart to the mystery and beauty of the developmentally disabled children in your community."

—REV. CARYL HURTIG CASBON

How the Lilies Grow is a tender, thoughtful account of one very courageous woman's struggle to meet the needs of her developmentally disabled child. I highly recommend this book to anyone trying to understand or cope with a similar circumstance."

—FRAN CHANGE, RN, BSN
Nursing Administrator, Volunteers in Medicine
Bend, Oregon

"It was a special pleasure for me to read *How the Lilies Grow.* I was the first social worker Barbara Munster contacted when she began looking for help for her five-year old developmentally disabled daughter, and later we were colleagues at the Golden Gate Regional Center. In more than twenty years as a social worker, I never met anyone more committed than Barbara to addressing the plight of the disabled. She is to be commended for this wonderful record of her perseverance, faith, and unconditional love."

—MARY E. GRAVES, MSW

"With honesty, vulnerability, and tremendous compassion, the author has described the demands and detailed experiences of a mother's ongoing care for her family and their developmentally disabled child. The look inside the family and the description of the societal context in which the family sought resources make *How the Lilies Grow* a unique contribution to the literature in this field. I would recommend this little volume as a part of a graduate-level training program attempting to prepare today's professional for a life of service and effective effort to this specific population."

—REV. RONALD A. MELVER, MDIV

How the Lilies Grow

Considering the Needs of a
Developmentally Disabled Child

by

Barbara Munster

AB

ABIDING BOOKS

CONDON, OREGON

HOW THE LILIES GROW
published by Abiding Books
© 2005 by Barbara Munster

International Standard Book Number: 0-9744284-8-5

Cover image by Barbara Munster
Cover design by Crown Marketing and Design
Interior design by Pamela McGrew.
Typeset by Katherine Lloyd

Matthew 6:28 is from *The Holy Bible,* King James Version.

Matthew 18:20 is from *The Holy Bible,* New International Version
© 1973, 1984 by International Bible Society, used by
permission of Zondervan Publishing House.

Printed in the United States of America

For information:
ABIDING BOOKS
P.O. BOX 243
CONDON, OR 97823

Library of Congress Cataloging-in-Publication Data

Munster, Barbara, 1938-
  How the lilies grow : considering the needs of a developmentally disabled
child / by Barbara Munster.
    p. cm.
  ISBN 0-9744284-8-5 (alk. paper)
  1. Munster, Barbara, 1938- 2. Moon, Karen Lenore. 3. Parents of children
with disabilities--United States--Biography. 4. Children with mental
disabilities--United States--Biography. 5. Children with mental disabilities--
United States--Family relationships. I. Title.
  RJ506.M4M86 2005
  649'.154'092--dc22
                                                          2005001185

05 06 07 08 09 10—10 9 8 7 6 5 4 3 2 1

To my mother,
who always saw the beauty in Lori.

Contents

Preface: *Consider the Lilies* 9

1. Good Soil 11

2. Learning to Cope 23

3. Not Alone 37

4. The Need for Change 51

5. The Way of Trust 65

6. The Burden of Choice 79

7. Through the Maze 95

8. A Living Death 111

9. Growing Above and Below 123

10. A Teacher and a Guide 139

Epilogue: *How They Grow* 151

Acknowledgments 157

About the Author 159

Consider the lilies of the field,
how they grow.

Matthew 6:28

Consider
the Lilies

In the Sermon on the Mount, Jesus tells us to *consider* the lilies, to think about them deliberately so we will learn something from them. Then He tells us what we are to be looking for—how they grow.

When I was a young child, my Sunday school teacher gave me a beautiful flower to take home and plant. I was thrilled, and ever since then it has fascinated me to watch flowers grow.

As an adult, I had three children. They were like the lilies of my own little field, and I spent years trying to provide them with all the things they needed to grow. Yet I might never have thought deeply about *how* they grew if one of them had not been developmentally disabled.

My purpose in writing this book is simply to consider how these special lilies grow. The undeniable fact is that our ability to meet the many needs of the developmentally disabled has not kept pace with their growing numbers. Perhaps this is because we as a society have not really *considered* them. In the belief that knowledge is the first step to change, I want to share with you what I have learned about meeting the needs of a special child.

How the Lilies Grow is written with deep compassion and appreciation for all those who are struggling to meet the special needs of the developmentally disabled. May you find comfort and encouragement from the story of one who has walked this road.

—Barbara Munster

chapter one

Good Soil

*A*lthough we don't often realize it, the conditions surrounding us in childhood have a profound influence on what we want out of life, how we go about getting it, and even if we do get it. Those circumstances are like the soil in which the seed of a life is sown, and to a great degree they set the boundaries of what is possible—or at least what we think is possible—at any given time. That was just as true for me as it would be for my disabled child.

❧

Even when I was very young, I realized that my family was somehow tainted. Nothing was ever said about it, but I knew that under the surface something was wrong.

My mother, Trudy, was the youngest of four children. She was born four years later than her next-oldest sibling, after Grandma had had several miscarriages, and she weighed only four pounds at birth. Mom really was the "baby" of the family, which perhaps explains why she was emotionally immature. She ended up pregnant at sixteen, and although there was a shotgun wedding, she continued to live with my grandparents after my sister Lou was born.

When she was nineteen, Mom met my father at a dance. Ted was a musician who played guitar in nightclubs and on the radio, gave music lessons, and occasionally worked as an appliance salesman. He was about ten years older than Mom, good looking, and apparently very persuasive, for my mother did whatever he wanted. Soon she was pregnant again, and in 1933 my sister Shirley was born. This time there was no wedding, for it seems Ted hadn't divorced his first wife. To make matters worse, he had a drinking problem and couldn't hold a job. My grandparents had to rescue my mother and sisters several times when they ran out of food, but Mom wouldn't leave Ted. He kept promising to marry her, and she kept believing him.

In 1936, Ted was about to stand trial for stealing money from his boss. Instead, he got a chance to start over in California.

A few years earlier, my Uncle Clyde had gone into business with my Aunt Ellen's husband, Mike. By 1936 the two had a successful camera shop in Oakland, and my grandfather talked Clyde into giving Ted a job. My parents moved from Missouri to California, and my grandparents, Alva and Cora, soon followed from Kansas.

I was born at home on February 4, 1937, three months after we moved to Oakland. Six months later, Ted lost the battle with the bottle and quit his job because "it wasn't good enough." With that, my grandfather told him to leave. Grandpa warned Ted that if he ever came around again, he would tell the police where they could find him. My parents were together less than five years, and I grew up not knowing my father.

Money was scarce during the Great Depression, but one thing hard times did for my family was to strengthen our sense of community and belonging. I was part of an extended family in which my aunts and uncles and grandparents treated me as if I were their own child. With my aunts and uncles close by, my grandparents, mother, sisters, and I lived together until 1943.

By then the United States was at war, my grandfather and mother had gone to work in the shipyards, and Uncle Clyde had enlisted in the Army. One of Uncle Clyde's hobbies was horseback riding, and since he needed a place to leave the horses while he was in the service, he bought a small farm in Livermore. The fall I entered first grade, Grandma and Shirley moved to the farm, and six months later the family decided that I should live there, too, while Grandpa, Mom, and Lou stayed in town. Nobody said anything to me about it. One day it was just time to move.

When I was older, I realized that Shirley and I had still needed supervision, while Lou, who was in the seventh grade, was old enough to stay alone while my grandfather and mother worked. At the time, however, I thought I was being punished by being sent away. Like my mother and grandfather, I enjoyed socializing, but Grandma rarely spoke, and Shirley spent all her time with her nose in a book. The nearest children lived a mile away. We didn't own a car, and I was too young to walk that far to visit. The first year on the farm was the loneliest time of my young life.

> *I thought I was being punished*
> *by being sent away.*

Things got better the following year, when my grandfather moved to the farm to be with us. Soon family and friends were pooling their gas rations and coming for supper almost every Sunday. Grandpa loved people and always had something to share, whether it was the Good Word or a chicken or rabbit from the farm. Between these visits, school, and chores, my life fell into a comfortable routine. Still, I was glad when the war ended and we moved back to town.

Three years later, my grandmother died. She had had health problems for many years, and I'm sure the work she did on the farm would have worn out even a healthy person. Part of Grandma's legacy to me was her conviction of the importance of education. She had graduated from a teacher's college and taught for several years before she married my grandfather. She was also very creative and could sew anything from scratch. In fact, she had wanted to be a milliner, but her folks thought that teaching was a more practical career. Grandma started giving me lessons on her treadle sewing machine when I was four.

Trudy was more like a beautiful older sister than a mother, and after my grandmother's death, my grandfather was the biggest influence in my life. Grandpa set strict standards for behavior, but he also answered all my questions and encouraged me to seek God's path for me. I was raised a Methodist, and every Sunday, rain or shine, we went to church. Struggling with feelings of being unclean and unworthy, I tried never to do anything wrong, and when I found clear guidelines in religion, I embraced them totally. Shirley often teased me about being a Goody Two-Shoes, but I really believed that if I followed what my grandfather and the church taught me, I would be a better person and my life would be easier.

All the while I was growing up, I desperately wanted to be like other children and have a father, but I was not allowed to ask questions about Ted. Once when I was in the fourth grade, we had a penmanship test that I did poorly on, but my teacher gave me a certificate anyway. "I know about your family," she said, "and I just want to help." Boy, did I feel tainted! When I said anything about my need, my grandfather would tell me that God was my father and that was enough. But it never was.

> *I desperately wanted to be like other*
> *children and have a father.*

Just as tainted soil affects how lilies grow, my perception of my family as incomplete and somehow tainted shaped me and affected the choices I made in life as I was growing up.

My mother remarried when I was sixteen. Bob was very controlling, and soon my sisters disappeared from my life. Lou went to Germany to teach school; Shirley dropped out of college and moved to San Francisco, where she soon fell in love and got married. After that, Bob focused his attention on me. He did his best to monitor my every move, telling me exactly what I could do, when to do it, and how long to do it. Because I so much wanted a father in the flesh, I tried very hard to please him by keeping quiet and being very submissive. If it hadn't been for Aunt Ellen, I might never have come to believe that I had the right to think for myself and express my opinions.

I also found emotional support in the church, and my social life increasingly revolved around church functions.

That's where I met Bill. We were both sixteen, and during high school we were both leaders in the Methodist church's youth programs. We enjoyed being leaders and were committed to living the kind of life exemplified by Christ—one of serving, caring for others, and sharing whatever we had. Everyone in the church just took it for granted that someday Bill would become a minister. Since that wasn't an option for women in the 1950s, they assumed that I would go into the field of social services.

When we started college in 1955, we did the expected. Bill went to San Francisco State College and declared a major in pre-ministerial studies. I went to UC Santa Barbara. I had wanted to go into social anthropology, but the field was just developing in the 1950s, and the nearest program was in Colorado. Studying psychology seemed to satisfy many of my emotional needs, so I combined it with my interest in social groups and settled on the field of social psychology.

After my freshman year, I transferred to UC Berkeley to be closer to Bill and his family. Right after I had gone off to college, my mother and stepfather sold their house and took an extended vacation in Mexico and Central America. As hard as it was for me to be around Bob, the lack of a home made me feel very insecure. Over the holidays the dorms closed down, and I had no place to stay until classes started again. All I could do was hope I'd be invited to someone's home. I longed to know that I belonged somewhere, and Bill's family always made me feel that way. They were totally welcoming and accepting of me.

On holidays they opened their home to me and let me know that, whatever the circumstances, I always had a place to stay.

> *I longed to know that*
> *I belonged somewhere.*

Halfway through our sophomore year, Bill and I decided to get married. Our minister thought it was a perfect match and encouraged us to take the next step. In addition, my circumstances made it seem like the practical thing to do. Although I had had a scholarship my first year, I had to work to pay for the second, and it had quickly become clear to me that I wasn't going to be able to survive economically or emotionally on my own, much less finish school.

As I considered myself deeply religious, I felt it would be a privilege to be a minister's wife. It was a secure, socially approved, well-defined role that I could embrace without reservation. Also, the thought of creating my own family unit thrilled me. I believed it would not only perpetuate the strengths I recognized in both our families, but also provide what my family had lacked. I envisioned our children flourishing in good soil.

I began my new life with Bill as an optimistic bride of twenty. Although we were both planning to complete our studies, on

September 22, 1958, nine and a half months after we were married, our first child was born. We named him Keith. He was the first grandchild and great-grandchild on both sides of the family, and love surrounded his birth and young life. Bill and I felt very blessed. We had boundless energy, and we truly believed we would be able to go to school, work, and raise a family all at the same time.

Then a few months after Keith's birth, Bill decided to drop out of college and take some time to "think about life." He had spent much of his young life on his family's farm in Alabama, and when he found out there was a cooperative dairy farm in Modesto, he decided we should move there. When I had lived on a farm as a child, I disliked the dirt and lack of social contact, so I didn't exactly relish the idea of moving to another one. But like most women in the late 1950s, I believed that a woman's place was with her husband, and I never questioned Bill's decision.

Two ministers with doctorates had founded the farm ten years earlier. They believed in nonviolence and wanted to live in a community with like-minded people. Gandhi's life had greatly influenced me, and I agreed with the principles of nonviolence, cooperation, and community. Still, I found it difficult to live on the farm.

Although I didn't lack social contact, I sure put up with a lot of dirt. We lived in a small two-bedroom wood building that had been built for temporary use during World War II. The floor consisted of wooden slats with splits so wide I could sweep out the dirt between the boards. The children in the commune looked like ragamuffins and rarely wore clean clothes.

When one of our farm family's infants was diagnosed with scurvy, I was furious. I thought there was no excuse for allowing a baby to experience such a terrible disease in modern times. People in the group believed they should be self-reliant, but I believed a child shouldn't have to suffer because the group wouldn't seek outside help.

My biggest struggle, however, was maintaining my sense of self in a situation where group rule was paramount. If the group made a decision we didn't buy into, we had to either go along with it or face ridicule. For example, the farm raised chickens to have eggs to eat. Each egg cost us eight cents to produce, but we could have bought them from the store for five. When Bill and I suggested that we stop raising chickens and buy our eggs at the store, they criticized us for being too businesslike. "You can't have a farm without chickens," they said.

I guess what they really meant was that we were too capitalistic, but I thought we were just being practical. I got to the point that I could no longer go along with the group when I knew there was a better way to do things. I found it intolerable for our family to live in such wretched conditions when we didn't have to. I wanted Bill to have an eight-to-five job, and I wanted to live in a nice house, go to church on Sundays, and socialize with friends occasionally. I had no doubt that the cultural values of mainstream America would provide a more fertile soil for family and community life than the doctrinaire ideals of a communal farm.

> *I got to the point that I could no longer go along with the group.*

This was a turning point for me. I began to question everything and became willing to challenge a system that didn't work. We finally took a hard look at what we were doing, and after many discussions, we decided to move back to the Bay Area and join mainstream society. Our cooperative farm experience had lasted six and a half months, but to me it seemed like years.

I urged Bill to go back to school, and he did. He never expressed a desire to return to preministerial studies and instead got a Bachelor of Arts degree. Times were good in postwar California, and after Bill graduated he got a job as a salesman for a plastics firm. He was quite good at what he did and quickly became a regional salesman. About a year after we returned to the city, we bought our first house, a fixer-upper in Albany.

Like nearly all marriages at the time, the division of labor in our home was based on gender. Bill brought home the money and handled outside chores; I took care of him, the children, and the house. To me that was just the way life was, and I really didn't mind, for I loved being a mother, caring for our home, and nurturing my family.

In my spare time I got involved in other activities. One of the first things I decided to do was to enroll in one college course per semester. I found this very empowering. It satisfied my desire to learn and at the same time moved me toward completing my bachelor's degree. My progress was slow, but that didn't matter. After all, I had most of my life ahead of me.

Around the same time we moved to Albany, we decided to conceive a second child, and on February 21, 1961, two weeks after my twenty-fourth birthday, I gave birth to a daughter. We named her Karen Lenore, and with her arrival we felt that our family was complete.

I believed that our family's foundation was solid, and I was very confident about our future. When Bill got use of a company car, we had two cars. Now that I had a way to get the kids around, we moved to the suburbs, where it was warmer. We bought a bigger house with a bigger yard in Alamo, a small town outside Walnut Creek. By 1964 we seemed to be the living picture of the "American dream." But things are not always what they seem, for by then I knew that something was very wrong with my daughter.

> *We seemed to be the living picture*
> *of the "American dream."*

chapter two

Learning to Cope

F*or me,* few things are as frustrating as knowing there's a problem but not why it exists or what to do about it. It was clear to me early in Karen's life that she had a problem, but it took me many years to discover what it was and many more to learn how to cope with it. During her first five years of life, I had more questions than answers, and that gave rise to strong emotions, including guilt, sadness, hurt, and fear. One of the most important things I had to learn to do was to channel these emotions into constructive actions.

For some reason, Karen was born susceptible to colds. Even though I had chosen natural childbirth and nursed her, she had her first cold when she was two weeks old, and she continued to be plagued with sniffles throughout infancy. I thought this predisposition might have been due to the fact that when I was in labor, the umbilical cord was around her neck for a short time. The attending doctor assured me that there would be no long-term effects, but I have always wondered if the stress compromised her immune system.

When Karen was about ten months old, she contracted a bad cold and ran a low-grade fever off and on for three months. Although her fever never peaked above 101 degrees, she couldn't keep food down and often woke up during the night. The doctor diagnosed flu and advised me to give her liquids until the fever subsided. During the day I fed her salted crackers to keep something in her stomach. She lost weight and most of her hair.

One night she awoke in great pain. When I picked her up, she arched her back and emitted a blood-curdling scream. I held her, walked with her, and rocked her, but nothing I did brought her comfort. I was so concerned that I took her to the pediatrician again. Over and over, I asked about the excruciating pain she had obviously experienced, but he seemed unconcerned. He insisted that she just had a pro-longed flu and that if I kept on doing what I was doing, eventually she would get better. In fact, he told me that the problem was mine, not Karen's. He said that I was overly anxious and that Karen felt my anxiety and reacted to it. I already felt devastated because I hadn't been able to relieve her pain; now I felt guilty as well.

> *He told me that the problem*
> *was mine, not Karen's.*

I remember reading once how the unemployment brought on by the Great Depression caused self-blame and self-doubt in men. They were expected to provide for their families, so when they lost their jobs, they believed they deserved it. In the 1950s and 1960s, something similar hap-pened to women. Mothers were expected to nurture and comfort their children, so anything that went wrong was apt to be attributed to poor mothering. Women who had inter-nalized these cultural expectations—and most of us had—would naturally blame themselves for the problem and feel guilty.

Although I did have feelings of guilt, I didn't get bogged down in them. In essence, guilt arises from a need to under-stand why something has gone wrong, so one way to move beyond it is to channel the feelings it creates into constructive

efforts to find the source of and possible solutions to the problem. Despite what the doctor said, I was convinced that
something was very wrong with Karen, and I was determined
to find out what it was and what I could do about it.

Frustrated by a lack of guidance, I changed doctors. Acting on
the advice and recommendation of friends and neighbors, I
took Karen to a wonderful family doctor whose practical help
gave me courage to use my intuition and common sense. I
placed her in a baby walker to keep her off the drafty floor, and
she stopped catching colds. Little by little she began to keep
her food down, and she began walking at fifteen months. But
though she finally seemed well again, I knew that something
was still wrong.

Shortly after the initial onset of the flu, I had noticed
Karen becoming more and more withdrawn. She would still
cry, but she stopped babbling and making other noises. It took
several weeks for me to realize that although she smiled, she
demanded nothing. When I smiled or cooed to her, she would
smile and respond with her eyes, but not with her voice.

Even when Karen cried, I couldn't connect it to any particular reason, except perhaps frustration. She never cried when
she was hurt or wet or hungry. One day when the new doctor
gave her a shot, he asked me why she didn't cry or flinch. "Can
she feel?" he asked. I didn't know whether she could or not.
Concerned, he told me to observe her closely.

A few days later, Karen toddled over to me with a shocked, pained look on her face. "What's wrong?" I asked her. After several minutes she cried out in pain. Examining her, I found burn marks beginning to show on her arm, and I realized she had fallen on the floor heater. My heart broke. I now knew she could feel, but I also knew she couldn't communicate. Now the question was *why*. Why couldn't she let me know what was wrong?

When Karen was eighteen months old, Grandpa Alva commented on the difficulty she had walking. She walked on her toes and had an awkward gait. I had already noticed the same thing and had talked with her doctor about it. He didn't know why she had this problem, so he referred me to a pediatric specialist in our area. In the mid-1960s, most tests for children were developmental, and based on the results of psychological testing, the specialist said that Karen was slow in developing but that she functioned within the normal range. He couldn't explain why her development was slow.

This doctor sent me to another specialist, who confirmed the diagnosis. He agreed that Karen obviously had some difficulties, but he didn't specify what they were, recommend any kind of treatment, or give me concrete ways I could help her. Instead, he suggested that I not worry, but just allow her to develop at her own pace.

The second doctor referred me to still another specialist, who conducted further tests, including one for phenylketonuria (PKU), a rare, inherited metabolic disease that results in mental retardation. Although testing for PKU is routine today, it wasn't regularly done until after the mid-sixties.

Despite the limited tests available then, Karen did eventually have an EEG. Her brainwaves showed abnormal activity. Although she had never had a noticeable seizure, there wasn't a single place in the outer area of her brain that didn't show some spiking.

> *There wasn't a single place in the outer area of her brain that didn't show some spiking.*

These results, along with Karen's nighttime screaming and prolonged illness, were enough to show that she had contracted encephalitis as a result of the flu. I finally had a diagnosis. Still, none of the specialists were able to tell me how I could help Karen. Left to find the answers on my own, I began to research, and I read everything I could get my hands on about flu encephalitis. I learned that it is an inflammation that enters a body weakened by some sort of flu and damages the lining of the brain. I also learned that one-third of those who contracted flu encephalitis recovered without side effects, one-third had minimal brain damage, and one-third became severely retarded.

I wept.

When I recovered from the shock, I realized there was still hope. By this time I had met another woman whose son was a few years older than Karen but had contracted flu encephalitis at about the same age. He had learning disabilities, but he didn't appear to be severely brain damaged. If the damage were minimal, Karen might be one of those who could function within the range considered normal.

I contacted the National Society for Crippled Children and Adults and asked for all the information they had on minimal brain injury. Most of it was about children with definite physical problems. Yet the only tangible thing I could get Karen's doctors to agree on was that though she was almost three years old, she could say fewer than five words, a sign that she was aphasic. (Aphasia is the impairment or loss of the power to use words as symbols of ideas.) Even so, no treatment was available for children under three.

When Karen was three, a good friend who was studying speech pathology at a nearby college encouraged me to have Karen's speech evaluated. I was eager to do so. Karen seemed to get frustrated because she wasn't able to say what she wanted. A clinic in East Oakland specialized in treating aphasic children, and I thought that with the one-on-one speech therapy it offered, Karen could learn to say more words and her frustration level would decrease. However, the clinic accepted only children who completely lacked verbal skills, and by now Karen could say about five words, so they didn't consider her aphasic. "Partial aphasia" was not then considered a diagnosis, so Karen didn't qualify for the clinic's special services.

Feelings of frustration led me to focus on finishing my college degree. I reached a point where I knew I could do nothing more to help Karen than what I was already doing. All I could do was protect her, love her day by day, and hope that the doctors were right that she would continue to learn at her pace. Even though I'd hit a wall, I somehow thought I could help her if I just knew more.

> *I somehow thought I could help*
> *her if I just knew more.*

Bill worked long hours and often traveled out of town during the week, so I had the freedom to pursue my education as long as it didn't interfere with my other responsibilities. Keith was now in school all day, and I hired a woman to care for Karen while I attended classes.

For eight and a half months my life was extremely hectic. Every day after I got Keith off to school, I drove Karen to the sitter's, which was twenty miles in the opposite direction from campus, and then drove to school. After classes, I reversed the process, finishing my one-hundred-mile commute by rushing home to be there when Keith arrived. Once home, I did the household chores, fixed dinner, put the children to bed, and then studied until all hours of the night. I got so little sleep that eventually my health was affected.

During final exams, I contracted a virus that caused me excruciating headaches and an upset stomach. I couldn't keep food down. I went to the doctor on Friday, and he advised me to rest, though he said I could take my final exams the following week. On Saturday, Bill was putting up a new fence with the help of a friend of ours. Carl was keenly aware of what was going on around him and sensitive to the needs of children. He volunteered to watch Karen, and I went back to bed, knowing that Karen would be safe with him. Sunday my mother came over so I could stay in bed, and on Monday I finished my exams.

I had attended undergraduate school for nine years, and I was proud to have a degree in social psychology. The subjects I had taken helped me understand the development of the psyche and gave me contacts in the field of developmental psychology, as well as in medical science. Taking classes had also given me a much-needed respite from the strain of trying to be a responsive parent to Karen when I couldn't find answers to my many questions. With my degree in hand, I felt encouraged and confident that I could cope better with Karen's situation.

Karen was an adorable child, but she was hyperactive. She was in constant motion, stopping only when she ate or slept. Since she couldn't talk, she would throw tantrums to get my attention. I quickly gained a keen intuition, and I got to the point that I instinctively knew what she wanted. The connection between us was so strong that I felt like a mother who was still attached to her newborn by the umbilical cord. Even with this almost telepathic communication, both of us were often frustrated, and she would wind up in tears.

I tried to teach Karen about heat, heights, and moving objects, but she didn't sense fear, and my scolding didn't bother her. I watched her every minute of the day so she wouldn't injure herself. I kept ipecac on hand in case she swallowed harmful liquids, kept doctors' numbers close at hand, and put special locks on cupboards and doors. As locks became part of our home decor, Karen became fascinated with them. Eventually, she could open all of them except those that needed a key or combination. She was a regular Houdini.

By trying to keep Karen safe, family members were sometimes either locked out of, or into, our home. No one could come and go freely, and of course, these methods weren't foolproof. Occasionally, family members would leave without letting me know so I could lock the door after them, and Karen would escape. Thank goodness for helpful and alert neighbors! If I telephoned or called to them from across our street, they would climb onto their roofs to let me know where she was hiding.

Outside, Karen would climb a tree and venture onto the branches, where she would hang by her fingertips until she was rescued. Getting her down presented major problems. We sawed off bottom limbs thinking this would deter her. No way.

Ingenuity was her strong suit, and she would always find a way to get up in the tree. If I was talking with a neighbor, planting flowers, or hanging wash, she would climb the tree and engage in death-defying behavior to get a reaction out of me.

I couldn't leave her in our fenced yard, as she could shinny up the seven-foot fence and drop over the other side before I could even cross the yard. Her agility was truly astounding, and she could climb any fence we built. She also was fearless, even though she'd fall on the other side of the fence. She got tremendous joy from teasing me by running and laughing as she went. She'd escape from the yard, run into the field, and hide among the wheat stalks. When I'd find her, she'd be giggling at the great fun she was having. I, of course, was not laughing.

Several friends surmised that if Karen were allowed to run whenever she wanted, she would eventually exhaust herself, so they took turns watching her as she ran. Unfortunately for them, the only one who got exhausted was the supervisor. Karen never got tired of running; she just got better at it.

> *Karen never got tired of running;*
> *she just got better at it.*

If we were out in the front yard, Karen would run into the street as fast as she could go. One time as I said good-bye to friends, she whipped past me into the street. I chased her, but I couldn't catch her, and a car knocked her down. Although the only injury she sustained was a stubbed toe, a frightened older couple got out of the car and stumbled to our front steps, where they fanned themselves while I brought them water. Meanwhile, elated by the commotion, Karen was ready to do it again. She knew her actions had caused me anxiety, so she wanted to repeat them until she got my undivided attention.

After a number of these episodes, I learned to keep my emotional reactions in check, as they just escalated her inappropriate behavior. I became adept at diverting her, if not at foiling her. I never knew how her next escapade would end, but over time I got so I could foresee what she might do next, and I would work with her, our family, and neighbors to ensure her safety. I also learned how to adapt to incidents as they occurred.

Even so, Karen continued to be a major challenge. She consumed my thoughts. No matter what I did, I thought about what she was up to or into. She still woke up three to five times a night, and as she now slept in a bed, she would get up and roam the house. The slightest sound of movement in her room woke me up. Exhausted, I searched for a way to make sure she wouldn't injure herself during the night. I ended up putting her in a special harness that was connected to a strap on her bed. The harness swiveled so that she could rotate 360 degrees but not get out of bed. At first I felt monstrous using the harness to contain her; then I felt comfort, knowing she was safe and that I could relax and sleep.

I found other ways to provide for her safety. There was a stuffed oversized chair in our family room, and when friends visited, Karen and I would sit wedged together in the chair, her body secure at my side. She could move her limbs around, and I could chat with friends without having to jump up and check on her. For safety outside, I used a spiral cord that expanded like a telephone cord, with a wristband that connected her wrist to mine. These safety restraints took some getting used to, and I was plagued with guilt the first time I tried a new one. But they allowed Karen a vast range of motion, and I was able to keep her out of danger.

By now Karen was "habit trained." She didn't tell me when she had to go to the bathroom, so I kept her dry by taking her at optimal times during the day. When she no longer had accidents in public, I could take her with me wherever I went. However, taking her out of the house had its own set of problems.

Grocery shopping with Karen was nerve-racking. She constantly grabbed items off shelves. I learned to steer the cart down the middle of the aisle while occupying her with word games. When we were standing in line, I held her hands so that she couldn't grab items from the checkout stand. Of course, the people around us muttered about my inability to control my child. Their comments hurt, but I didn't have the energy to explain our situation. I couldn't have explained it in any event, for I wasn't able to talk without Karen jumping around and causing a greater disturbance. No one seemed to have a clue about what we were dealing with.

chapter three

Not Alone

Lilies do not grow alone; they grow in clumps. In the same way that one lily needs the support of others to thrive, so meeting the needs of developmentally disabled children means meeting the needs of the families who care for them. The help and support of others is an absolute necessity for such families. This support can come from God, family, professionals, friends, support groups, and public programs and institutions. Ideally, it comes from all these sources, for these families need to know that they are not alone.

Although I could understand why strangers would react neg-
atively to Karen, it really hurt me to have family members
reject her. One day my stepfather called me to tell me that I
shouldn't bring Karen to their home. In fact, he told me that
I shouldn't take her out in public at all. Bob's call came out of
the blue after I had been struggling for months to find out
what was wrong with Karen and what I could do to help her.
If there was ever a time I needed the support and understanding of my family, this was it.

I never knew if my mom was aware of what Bob said to
me, but at the time I was angry and devastated that grandparents would reject their grandchild. Keith was Bob's
favorite, and he and my mother took great joy in his visits.
I didn't see how Bob could accept Keith, but not Karen.
Fortunately, my sister Lou had just returned to the Bay Area,
and she helped me know how to respond. She had several
preschoolers and a listening ear, and she advised me to just
ignore Bob's comment and act as if he had never made it. She
said that he spoke from ignorance and suggested I forgive
and help him learn to understand Karen.

This was a major lesson for me in learning how to channel
my emotions into constructive behavior. When I desperately
needed encouragement myself, I had to reach out to others. I
encouraged Bob and Mom to visit us and spend time with
Karen, and little by little Bob learned to love her as a special

grandchild. In the process, they also learned how to support our efforts to help her.

Bill and I included Karen in all family events. We even went camping until she was five years old. One time when we were traveling the Avenue of the Giants, Bill decided to stop the car. Physically and emotionally exhausted from watching Karen, I asked him to keep an eye on the children while I went off to sit by myself on a hillside. There I prayed for patience and help in caring for Karen, and after a while I felt peace. When I returned to my family, to my amazement I found them picking and eating blackberries in the safety of a small apple grove hidden away from the highway among the redwoods.

I had never before felt that it was safe to leave Karen with Bill because he would often forget that he was supposed to be watching her and turn his attention to something else. Even now, his attention was focused on enjoying the berries, not on watching the children. What was different was that I now knew for certain that God was watching over Karen. I was grateful for His providential care, and from that moment on I knew I was not alone.

> *I now knew for certain that God*
> *was watching over Karen.*

This assurance helped me take the next step in my ongoing search for answers for Karen. Up until this time, every doctor and evaluator I had talked to had stated that Karen functioned in the normal range and had told me to treat her as I would a normal child. I now knew that waiting for her to develop at her own pace wasn't the answer. I was convinced that she had special needs, though I didn't always know exactly what they were.

One thing I did know was that I could not sit back and do nothing, passively waiting for her life to evolve. I had learned that stimulation therapy helped children gain skills, and if that would give her the help she needed, I wanted to provide her with it.

When Karen was five years old, I heard about Doman-Delcato therapy, which had been in use for brain-damaged children since 1956. This therapy was based on the theory of sensory integration that Dr. Glen Delacato developed in his work with brain-damaged children and on the theory of neurologically based movement ("patterning") that Dr. Robert Doman developed in his work with children with learning disabilities.

The underlying assumption of this method was that it was possible to "retrain" the injured parts of the brain. The theory was that the brain could develop new pathways by having the body revert to the movements of the fetus in the womb and then move progressively through the stages of movement infants experience as they grow.

The nearest clinic that supported this therapeutic method was in San Diego. Our pediatrician made the referral, and a short time later we flew there for an evaluation. At the clinic we were informed that Karen's condition was typical of brain-injured children but that tests were needed to determine the extent of injury.

Meanwhile, the clinic staff provided us with literature on the treatment and prescribed an intensive three-month program consisting primarily of patterning. The prognosis for Karen's development, they said, would depend on how well we implemented the prescribed therapy and how closely we adhered to the regime. Finally, I had something tangible to do! I was excited about the therapy and full of hope.

> *I was excited about the therapy*
> *and full of hope.*

In order for the damaged portion of her brain to have a chance to reconnect, Karen had to creep and then crawl before she eventually returned to walking. This meant that she was not permitted to walk at any time during the first six months. For me, this was the most difficult part of the therapy; forcing her to crawl seemed more than I could deal with. Except for when she was sitting at the table or doing a specific exercise, she had to wear kneepads and a special harness at all times. But I was willing to try anything, and with tears in my eyes and a lump in my throat, I put the harness on her.

Karen's program began early each day and didn't end until after dinner. For the first six months, I spent seven hours each day on her various exercises. Patterning alone required the efforts of three volunteers, three times a day, seven days a week. These volunteers would move Karen's arms, legs, and head simultaneously for fifteen minutes during each session.

The remainder of the day was devoted to different activities, including encouraging her to creep through a crawl box; putting peanut butter on the roof of her mouth so she would have to exercise her tongue to remove it; providing all her food in small pieces so she would have to use her finger and thumb to pick them up; having her breathe into a special mask for a short while several times a day to cause her blood capillaries to dilate; and practicing word recognition.

Six volunteers came to our home every single day of the week. Karen began playing special games with them, with each game unique to a particular volunteer. She gained many wonderful friends who continued to visit her and remained concerned about her for many years.

One friend gave us an adorable black Labrador-Samoyed puppy to encourage Karen to crawl. Keith named him Sam. A beautiful, mild-tempered dog that resembled a black bear cub, Sam was the perfect playmate for Karen. We didn't concern ourselves with her playing rough with him, as his fur was quite thick and he had a gentle personality. Sam became Karen's constant companion, though Keith became his master. We all fell in love with Sam, and he seemed to know how important he was to our family.

Sam was just one part of a support group that began to coalesce around us. Our community supported us by running articles in our local newspaper asking for help locating volunteers. A local church sponsored weekly volunteers, and the community at large provided substitutes for Sundays. We lived in a fishbowl. I could never relax or allow household chores to pile up, as volunteers arrived every three hours. Over a period of one and a half years, three hundred people came to our home. Fishbowl life aside, I felt greatly energized. I had a support system in place, and I was taking action. I no longer felt like life's victim.

Every three months we flew to the San Diego clinic for reevaluation and a set of changes to Karen's program. We met other families with brain-injured children, and when we returned home from the clinic, we began to meet with the ones who lived closest to us. This support group gave me even more strength, as it allowed me to compare notes and share my feelings of exhaustion. We gave one another the encouragement and stamina we needed to continue the program, and after a few meetings we began to discuss starting a clinic nearby so we wouldn't have to fly down to San Diego.

By pooling our energies and talents, within six months we raised enough money to hire a trained person to open a clinic in Mountain View. I was thrilled to be part of such a constructive and beneficial project, and I saw clearly that practical group undertakings like this were essential to providing families with the resources they needed to raise a developmentally disabled child.

When we began to see changes take place in Karen, my enthusiasm soared. Within the first three months of therapy, she recovered much of her skin sensation. I had been told to use "Sister Kenney's treatment." This therapy was named after Sister Elizabeth Kenney (the "Sister" designation was an Australian military term), who developed the first treatment for paralytic polio in the early twentieth century. It consisted of rubbing a salt-brine solution on much of Karen's skin for about ten minutes three times a day.

> *When we began to see changes take place in Karen, my enthusiasm soared.*

At first Karen would laugh when I did this. But as the weeks went by, she began to squirm. After three months, she would cry. She was obviously feeling pain, so I discontinued the treatment. When the doctor at the clinic tested Karen's Achilles tendon, she responded to the pain. Even though there was a slight delay in her response, it was obvious that she could feel and react to pain.

Yet something was still missing. When most children get hurt, they remember the situation that caused the pain and avoid repeating it. Not Karen. Having been with little or no skin sensation for so long, she had absolutely no fear of danger. It meant nothing to her for me to tell her not to do something because she might get hurt. I finally realized that Karen's behavior indicated that she had no short-term memory. She did, however, appear to have long-term memory and would remember things that were in some way important to her.

To me, the questions became "What triggers her long-term memory?" and "How can I make sure something is important enough to her that she will remember it?" I began observing and making notes of when Karen remembered and when she didn't. Gradually it became clear that if something had an emotional component for her—not necessarily for me, but for her—she would retain the information. Now the challenge became to learn how I could help her *want* to remember the skills she needed.

Though Karen's therapy helped initially, over time her progress slowed until after about eighteen months of the seven-day-a-week routine, we could discern no change at all. Karen was also showing signs of resistance. At the beginning of the program she was in therapy for ten hours a day. Later the time was reduced to six hours, but that was still a tremendous amount of time for a child to be forced to participate in planned activities.

One morning while she was eating breakfast, Karen accidentally dropped her spoon. I told her to be more careful, but I noticed she had a very quizzical look on her face. In a couple of minutes she dropped her spoon again. This time, however, a grand mal seizure followed, and I rushed over to keep her from injuring herself. I felt so bad that I had scolded her when her actions had obviously been involuntary.

I called her pediatrician, who immediately advised me to take her to Children's Hospital for an overnight evaluation. The EEG showed constant seizure activity, so phenobarbital was prescribed. When she was released from the hospital, Karen was very drowsy and unable to walk without falling. She seemed to be affected from her waist down and had no control over her legs. When she didn't improve, it was clear that she had either suffered further brain damage or was having a negative reaction to the medication.

> *Karen's system just couldn't take the constant demands of therapy anymore.*

The doctor changed her medication, and the next one left her sleeping most of the time. Eventually she was put on Dilantin, which seemed to have the fewest side effects. Her EEG showed constant seizure activity, and I was told she would have to be on some kind of antiseizure medication for the rest of her life.

I tried to understand what had happened. It seemed to me that Karen's system just couldn't take the constant demands of therapy anymore. She did not want to crawl. She was tired of being manipulated, and she had signaled this by her increasing resistance to the therapy. In hindsight, I believe I should have responded to her moods and modified her therapy so she wouldn't be under such terrible strain. Possibly then her body might not have reacted with a grand mal seizure. To this day, I have never seen her have another one.

After this episode, I called the Doman-Delcato clinic for advice. I told them that the doctors had put Karen on anti-seizure medication, and they recommended that we stop the therapy and take her to the headquarters in Philadelphia for a thorough evaluation by a pediatric neurosurgeon. Within two weeks we flew to New York and drove to the clinic in Philadelphia.

The trip was memorable for many reasons. First, the big challenge was to confine our very active Karen when we were in public places. Fortunately, Karen loved to fly, and much to our delight, she was an angel during the flight.

What we learned from our consultation was that seizure activity often occurs when brain waves come in contact with scar tissue as the brain forms new pathways. Karen might benefit from further therapy, but she might also have frequent seizures. The doctor told us not to fear the possibility of seizures because proceeding in spite of them could potentially help her function at a higher level. He couldn't guarantee us that she would do this, but he felt confident that she would. He assured us that seizures would not cause further damage and recommended that she be taken off all medication.

We left the clinic not knowing what to do. The doctor at home said Karen had to be on medication, while the doctor at the clinic said she should be taken off medication and continue therapy.

With questions in our heart, we drove back to New York. By the time we arrived, it was dinnertime, and not knowing the Queens district of New York, we stopped at a restaurant that served family style. Since we had Karen with us, we thought the casual atmosphere would be best, but the dinner was anything but casual. Karen was her usual hyper self, and I couldn't keep her focused on eating. When she got bored, she began undressing herself. It became a major ordeal just to keep her dressed, much less eat dinner. All of the customers nearby were aware of our situation and attempted to ignore us. I only remember finishing my soup. Exhausted, we left the restaurant to relax in our hotel room until it was time to catch our plane.

By the time we arrived home, we had decided that a change was in order for everyone. For a year and a half, our entire family life had revolved around Karen's therapy program. Everything we did depended on the set of exercises Karen needed to complete. All of us were very tired, and Karen's progress seemed to have ground to a halt.

Before therapy, Karen had been able to say only a few words. Now she was able to use one thousand words. Although she couldn't use articles, she could combine verbs, nouns, and voice inflection to express a complete thought: "Dog eat?" "Want food?" She could follow directions, and now that she could talk, she no longer exhibited the frustration she once had. I was glad that she could communicate at least some of her thoughts. She could also identify a few printed words, which told me that she could relate meaning to words. She appeared to be able to learn and liked to learn, but she had little or no immediate retention.

The big unknown now was how independent Karen might become, and my thoughts focused on how I could help her gain basic social and survival skills. I was consumed with how best to help her, but I didn't know where to find guidance. I did know that the earlier she got help, the greater the results would be, and I wanted to do everything possible to provide positive and necessary intervention.

> *By now I was fully aware that I could no longer think of Karen as "normal."*

By now I was fully aware that I could no longer think of Karen as "normal." She still required constant supervision. She still loved to play hide-and-seek and try to outsmart adults, and she would still scale the fence and take off. As I reviewed the results of therapy, I saw that another problem had arisen from her exercise program. She had come to like being the center of attention and was very manipulative in her attempts

to stay there. When she wasn't the center, she did inappropriate, silly, or dangerous things.

After much soul-searching, I realized that it was not healthy
for Karen or the rest of the family for her activities to take
precedence over everything else. The therapy had had a won-
derfully stimulating effect on her brain, and she had obviously
gained some important skills. Through the exercises she had
also become very strong and physically fit. But now it was
time to try something else. If something didn't change, no one
in our family would ever have a chance to live normally.

chapter four

The Need for Change

In my view, a "normal" family is one in which each member is equally important and everyone works together for the benefit of all. But how is it possible to have a normal family life when one member of the family is not normal? The inescapable fact was that our family could not function in that way. An important part of meeting the needs of the developmentally disabled is to recognize the need for change and to respond to it in the best way you know how.

By this time, I had become acquainted with many parents who had a disabled child, and what I saw—and was beginning to experience myself—was that the mother became totally consumed with taking care of the child. Often she neglected her husband, and her other children had to do without her nurturing and loving support. The family's energy and finances were skewed toward the child's needs, and the stress often destroyed the family unit. At that time, more than 90 percent of all fathers of disabled children abandoned their families, either physically or emotionally. I didn't want our family to become a statistic.

Yet all our activities did in fact revolve around the most demanding member of our family. Karen's needs consumed my waking time and a good part of my sleeping time as well. I consciously tried to make sure I didn't neglect my husband and son, but I would get caught up emotionally and focus on the demands of my disabled daughter.

I wanted to be proactive, not reactive, and to balance our

> *Karen's needs consumed my waking time and a good part of my sleeping time as well.*

family life so that Karen was not always at the forefront. I wanted to find a healthy balance that would help Karen but also allow me to be a good mother to Keith and a good wife to Bill. I didn't want Karen's need for constant supervision to outweigh my other responsibilities any longer.

Although Bill and I had thought that two children were a perfect size for a family, we now discussed having a third. We felt that Keith would grow up less scarred if he had a normal brother or sister to relate to and that another child might help us gain perspective as a family. I thought that having to meet the basic needs of another child would *force* me to react to Karen in a different, healthier way. We didn't even consider the possibility that we might have another disabled child, for Karen's problems were not genetic, but the result of illness. When I became pregnant, we were elated.

Bill was still away from home during the week, and I still handled all the domestic chores. Although I certainly knew it would be taxing to have another child, at the time I didn't realize how difficult the pregnancy would be and how much the added stress of caring for the baby would force me to grow and change.

During my fifth month of pregnancy, there were some complications, and my obstetrician advised me to rest with my legs elevated. It was a huge challenge to figure out how I could do this and still watch Karen. I ended up corralling her in the dining room by blocking all the doorways and then sat with my legs on the seat of a chair in front of me. I had toys strewn everywhere so she could play.

Another challenge was to occupy my brain, as sometimes I was bored out of my mind. I began hooking rugs. Rug hooking didn't require much attention, but it did give me a way to focus my energy and reduce my tension. Even though it gave me a sense of accomplishment, after the baby was born I never wanted to see another hooked rug again.

Shortly before my due date, my obstetrician told me that the baby was not situated properly in the birth canal. It was oblique, its head resting against my pelvis. Anxiety plagued me during the last few weeks of my pregnancy. When I began labor, I would have to get to the hospital immediately, as pressure on the baby in its present position could cause it severe trauma.

My water broke while we were visiting friends on August 11, 1967. We made a mad dash to the hospital, and shortly after we got there I underwent a cesarean section. I never knew what a "peaches-and-cream complexion" was until I saw our beautiful baby girl. She didn't have a blemish on her. We named her Lesli Anne.

> *I felt I had given 110 percent in the game*
> *of life, and I was ready to cash in my chips.*

Physically and emotionally exhausted, I felt as though all I wanted to do was sleep and never awaken. I felt I had given 110 percent in the game of life, and I was ready to cash in my chips. I relaxed into pure peace, savoring the sense that I could now go. I drifted off, seeming to leave my body. Then, I heard a voice in my head say, "This is not your time."

At that moment, I seemed to return to my body, and I became aware that a nurse was saying, "Stay awake. You must stay awake."

"Okay," I mumbled reluctantly. I was back in the game.

Though I was thrilled with my beautiful baby, recuperating from the C-section, caring for Lesli Anne, and providing for Karen and Keith was too much for me to handle by myself. I enlisted the aid of family and friends. They handled the chores they felt comfortable doing, while I did the rest. Keith, now nine, was a major help. Everyone was delighted to help me with the baby, but no one felt comfortable caring for Karen unless I was present. As a result, Lesli Anne was bottle-fed even though I had wanted to breast-feed her.

By now Karen was six and a half. Thinking that she might benefit from being around other children, I enrolled her in preschool. With her gone for part of the day, I was freer than before but still overwhelmed with responsibilities. Except for the time she spent at school, Karen was always near me, so I couldn't spend much time getting to know Lesli Anne. I ached to cuddle and coo to her without others always present, but I also didn't want Karen to feel that she was being replaced.

I was also deeply concerned about Lesli's safety. Karen needed continuous supervision around the baby. She would try to pick her up and bring her to me whenever she cried. To divert her, I encouraged her to talk to the baby instead.

One day when Lesli was six months old, Karen ran to me and said, "Baby talk."

"Oh, that's nice," I said as I went on cleaning up the kitchen.

Karen pulled and tugged at me. "Baby talk. Baby talk," she said.

Finally I went with her. Karen stood over Lesli and said, "Say Mama." Sure enough, Lesli said, "Mama." Needless to say, I was stunned! Thanks to Karen, Lesli had said her first word at six months—on cue! I laughed and then hugged Karen, praising her for the good job she had done.

When Karen was seven, I enrolled her in classes for the trainable mentally retarded at public school. She stood by the window every day, eagerly awaiting the yellow school bus. She loved the bus ride. However, in class she refused to sit in her assigned chair or to respond to her name. Her teacher telephoned me and asked if she knew her name. Of course, I told her. She always responded when I called her. Could the sound of the letter *k* be a problem? No. She could say "Keith." However, she never said her own name.

That evening, I asked Karen why she didn't sit in the seat with the name Karen on it. She gave no sign that she heard me. Later that evening, I talked with my friend Wilma, who suggested I ask Karen which name she liked, her first name or her middle name.

The next night I told Karen that her full name was Karen Lenore Moon. I told her how her dad and I had chosen the names just for her.

"Which name would you like me to call you?" I asked. "Karen? Or Lenore?"

To my surprise, she quickly answered, "La-ore."

The following day, I sent a note to the school saying that Karen wanted to be called Lenore. Her teacher called me again, this time to tell me that the sign on Karen's seat had been changed to "Lenore" and that Lenore happily sat there when she asked her to.

Karen's classmates, however, had trouble saying "Lenore," so they shorted it to "Lor." And, as children often do, they added the sound of *y* to the end and called her "Lori." From then on, she was Lori at home as well as at school. I was so happy that she now had a name she enjoyed and would say.

Three months later, the school psychologist called me to request a home visit. When she arrived, she quizzed me about the reason for Lori's name change. I said I felt Lori had a right to be called whatever name contributed to her comfort. However, the psychologist said that Lori must be autistic because "only autistic children change their names." She had obviously come with an agenda, and her statement stunned and infuriated me.

At that time most people assumed that autistic children didn't relate at all to people, much less animals. They lived in their own internal world. Karen, however, was a very affectionate child who loved people and dogs. I had also spent a great deal of time studying art and play therapy in order to help her benefit in every possible way from what was then known about how to help disabled children.

> *The psychologist said that Lori must be autistic because "only autistic children change their names."*

The psychologist who came to our home didn't know the first thing about Lori and hadn't taken any time to find out before she came out with her diagnosis. She hadn't come to contribute to my child's well-being, but to check out the home in which Lori lived to accumulate "evidence" to support what she already believed. She not only said that Lori was autistic, but that I had obviously played a major role in making her so. In the 1960s, most people just assumed that a child's problems were the result of poor mothering. I showed the psychologist the door, and I never heard from her again.

As a result of her visit, though, I searched my soul, as well as my intellect, for answers to my questions. Why had Karen disliked her name? I finally concluded that during her year and a half of therapy, she had spent her entire day with people who said, "Karen, it's time for this" and "Karen, do that." She associated her name with the therapy, and when she had begun to resist the exercises, she also resisted responding to her name.

In many ways children with mental disabilities grow just as children without them do. A person's identity changes over time, and as they grow and change, many people signal a new stage in life by changing their name in some way. A child stops using a nickname as he gets older; a man drops Jr. when his father dies; a woman takes her husband's name when she marries. Lori was no different. She had her own unique identity that was changing as she experienced new things. When the name "Karen" no longer matched who she was, she stopped responding to it, and she became Lori.

After Lori had been in school for a year, it was clear that she was not learning the skills she needed to function independently. In my search for the best educational solution for her, I discovered that training for brain-injured children was almost nonexistent. Repetition was the only method of teaching the developmentally disabled in public schools. This discovery was very disheartening, as I knew I couldn't be Lori's lifeline forever.

Then I learned about California's Regional Center System, a nonprofit agency established to coordinate resources and provide diagnostic services for disabled children so that families like ours would not have to cast about, hither and yon, to find doctors, diagnosticians, and services. The first two centers opened in 1966. One, the Children's Hospital Regional Center, served the Los Angeles area; the other, the Golden Gate Regional Center (GGRC) served the five counties of the San Francisco Bay Area.

Bill and I arranged for an appointment at the GGRC in the hope that it could furnish us with, or at least recommend, a better educational program for Lori. When I telephoned the center, the staff asked for a brief history and requested the release of Lori's medical records. They would call us back after they had received and reviewed the records.

Within a month, a social worker and physician visited us to observe Lori in our home. Keith was now ten years old and in the fourth grade; Lesli Anne was two. As the two professionals observed the children and asked questions, Lori decided to be extra silly. She went into the bathroom and then trotted back to the living room, where she squeezed toothpaste all over her toothbrush and the floor. I took the paste and toothbrush from her and redirected her to playing with puzzles, as Lesli was doing.

Lesli solved her puzzle first, and Lori messed it up. I mildly reprimanded her. She continued her hyperactive behavior, so I held her hand while I finished talking with our visitors. I told them that the local school was inadequate to teach brain-injured children and that I wanted to find a school where Lori could learn appropriate life skills. After a thirty-minute visit, they left, telling me they would be in touch.

The next week, the social worker telephoned me with the results of their evaluation. After reviewing all the records, the doctor had recommended Lori for a school program, excellently rated, in Watsonville. Funded as a federal pilot program, it included using farm animals as teaching tools and also relied on the latest techniques for training staff. The doctor assured me that the program was perfect for Lori's special needs.

There was one catch. Lori would have to move to a residential home in Watsonville. There was only one such program in the area and only one opening. While funding to subsidize her home was currently available, it might not be in two weeks. To take advantage of this educational opportunity, Lori would have to move into the home within the week. The center needed a decision from Bill and me within twenty-four hours, and if we accepted the placement, Lori would have to move in two days.

My head was spinning. How could I do this? Some people thought disabled children should be placed in institutions; others thought they should be cared for at home. I personally believed that everyone deserves a place in a family, including the disabled. No matter how difficult Lori was to care for, I had never considered her living anywhere but at home. Bill and I had never discussed her living elsewhere. I had just been searching for a better educational program. Grief-stricken and emotionally overwhelmed, I agonized over what to do. All of this had happened too quickly. How could I make a decision in twenty-four hours?

I spoke with many friends that day, asking for suggestions and advice—anything that would help with the decision. I talked with a counselor and with a loving aunt, but I found no relief from the grief I felt. I gained some peace by reading the stories from Bruno Bettelheim's study of Israeli children who lived in a kibbutz without their natural parents. These children seemed to have no major personality problems as a result of being raised by other adults.

That night, Bill and I discussed the situation at length. Tomorrow was the deadline. The program was the best California offered for brain-injured children, and Bill believed that Lori would have a chance at learning if she lived at Watsonville. I knew in my heart that this was so, but still I cried. So did Bill. We'd have to sign release papers, but I didn't want to. This change was too big, too sudden. I didn't want to send Lori away to live with strangers—not yet, not ever. Bill wanted to sign.

> *I didn't want to send Lori away to live with strangers—not yet, not ever.*

The next morning we agreed to send Lori to Watsonville. We told Keith, of course, explaining how we thought Lori would gain skills that would help her get along better in life. He seemed to understand, though he, too, was sad and said how much he would miss her. We told Lesli Anne as well, even though she was too young to understand. We told Lori that she would be living in a new place, but that we would visit and she could come home for visits. She would meet lots of new people, make new friends, and learn new skills. Though she didn't understand, she grinned her marvelous grin, her mouth wide open.

Bill called the center and told them that we would sign the papers and drive to Watsonville that weekend. With tears rolling down my cheeks, I prepared name labels for Lori's clothes. On Saturday, Bill, Keith, Lesli, and I took Lori to her new home. She seemed excited to be going to a new place. I could hardly speak from emotion. Keith talked to Lori in the backseat, and I saw him struggle with his emotions as well. Bill was silent and kept his eyes on the road as he drove.

The older couple that operated the home greeted us at the door and showed us around the residence. It seemed as excellent as the staff at the center had said it was. Maybe we *had* made the right decision for Lori. Still, I moved as if in a dream. I know I responded to that caring couple. I know I hugged and kissed Lori good-bye. I know that the woman told us not to visit Lori until six weeks had passed in order to give her time to adjust. This was news, and it seemed particularly cruel coming as it did at the last moment. But I had signed, and I had no choice but to agree. Six weeks. I felt as though one of my arms or legs had been amputated.

When we arrived home, I went into my room to rest. What had we done? I deeply loved Lori and wasn't ready to give her up. Had I done the best I could, or had I thrown her to the wolves? I wanted Lori to have this chance to gain skills, but in my heart there was a void, and I felt I had abandoned her. I had felt abandoned as a child, and I didn't want that for Lori. I wept and wept and wept.

Many sleepless nights followed. I was angry with Bill. I was angry with myself. As the next few weeks dragged by, I talked with friends, family, a counselor, Bill, and Keith. I reread Bettelheim's stories. Some days, I couldn't stop crying. I felt bereft.

Then one day as I was watching Lesli play, it struck me. For the first time ever, I was enjoying Lesli without having to check on Lori. I no longer had to keep all the doors locked. Keith could go in and out as he pleased, and I could go into the yard and do whatever I wanted, even sunbathe, without worrying that Lori would escape. Our family could eat dinner without constant interruptions. I smiled.

Lori was now living in a very good place, one where she would gain skills she desperately needed. I missed her terribly, but there was no reason for me to feel guilty. My goal had been to take action to help Lori, and I had. I had played the cards life dealt me the best I knew how.

> *I had played the cards life dealt me*
> *the best I knew how.*

Karen at 13 months, after she had lost most of her hair

Karen playing in the backyard

Karen at 6, with baby sister Lesli

Lori at 11, enjoying time at home

Lori, Lesli, and Keith, Christmas 1972

Lori at 12, chatting with her favorite grandmother

At 19, Lori won a medal in roller skating

Lori learning to ski at age 27

Lori (left) running in the Special Olympics at age 17

Lori at 33, singing along with the player piano

Lori dressed up for Keith and Jenny's wedding, 1986

I receive the John R. May Award in 1987. Left to right: Jenny, Lori, Keith, me, and Lesli

Lori rafting with Keith and Jenny

Keith escorts Lori at Gregg's and my wedding, 1990

Lori enjoying her Christmas presents, 1992

Lori at 41. Since 1997, Lori has lived in community with supervision. Throughout her life, this has been my constant hope for her, and I pray that she can continue to do so until her life on earth is over.

chapter five

The Way of Trust

*T*rusting in God, in others, or even in your own judgment can be a scary thing. Learning to trust required me to make decisions in the midst of confusing and stressful circumstances, and it wasn't easy to act on what I knew to be right and true regardless of the outcome. Yet tapping into my inner wisdom and then stepping out in faith was essential to meet not only Lori's needs, but also my own.

❧

Despite my sadness and anger, we had made the right decision for Lori, and she made progress in the three years she was in the residential program in Watsonville. Then one day while I was at work, I received a call from her program manager telling me that Lori had gone "berserk." I asked what she meant. Evidently, Lori had become angry when she was taken to the toilet and had picked up the toilet lid, thrown it down, and broken it.

The manager said that Lori had to be taken to the county hospital's psychiatric ward immediately. However, she could not admit her to the psychiatric ward without my permission because Lori was not yet eighteen. Shocked, distraught, and angry, I absolutely refused. Before, I would not have questioned what a person in a position of "authority" told me I had to do with regard to Lori. Now I was beyond that.

I had always known that I didn't have all the answers, and I had looked to "experts," only to find that most not only didn't have the answers either, but also didn't care about what was best for Lori. I had to trust my own judgment, and I insisted that the manager call a physician for an evaluation before taking such a drastic step.

Still, I wondered what could have caused Lori to act in such an inappropriate manner. After three days of struggling to get answers, I was exhausted from stress, and my face broke out with acne. As I was on the way to my office, one of my coworkers asked what was upsetting me. I told him. He asked me questions about Lori and then told me about a meditation group he belonged to. The members got together weekly to pray for various people and concerns. They planned to meet that afternoon, and he asked permission to present Lori's case. I agreed, comforted that he cared and would take the time to show it.

That same afternoon, around four, I felt a huge warm surge through my body, accompanied by an encompassing sense of well-being. I felt as though I were being held in hands covered with goose down. Something deep inside assured me that everything would be all right. After work, I told Bill about the experience. While speaking to him, I glanced in the mirror and saw that the acne blemishes had disappeared. I was speechless. I had just experienced the power of healing through prayer.

> *I felt a huge warm surge through my body, accompanied by an encompassing sense of well-being.*

As a child and young adult, I had prayed many times, which for me usually meant closing my eyes, folding my hands, and thanking God or asking Him for something. It was a ritual, not an experience, for I had never learned to listen to God or to trust Him. Of course, I'd heard and read stories about healing and miracles, and I believed they could happen. I just didn't believe they would happen to *me*.

Now part of me knew that through the power of the prayers of the people in my coworker's meditation group, a miracle had happened—for me. I had experienced the truth and power of Matthew 18:20: "Where two or three come together in my name, there am I with them." Before this I had *believed* that through Jesus, and thus God, anything was possible. But now I had *experienced* it.

That evening my coworker telephoned to ask about Lori. I told him I hadn't heard any more about her situation. I described my experience and thanked him and his group for the miraculous healing, but added that the healing I desperately wanted was for Lori. He asked me more questions about her and told me the group would meet again that evening and pray specifically for her.

The next morning I didn't receive my daily emergency call from the residential staff. Later that day, though, they called to tell me that a doctor had seen Lori and taken a blood sample. The test showed that her blood was toxic from her anticonvulsing medication. The doctor asked me to bring her home while she withdrew from the meds, and the residence agreed that she could return when her withdrawal symptoms stopped. I arranged to pick Lori up.

Within three days after Lori got home, her skin changed from yellow to a normal, healthy pink. Her body no longer smelled acrid, and her dark stools changed to a more normal color. Thrilled to be home, she spent her time coloring and playing with her toys. Her tiny writing went from squiggly chicken scratch to large, smooth strokes as her body was cleansed of the medications. She stayed at home for one week to be certain that her system was rid of the toxicity.

Although this problem was resolved and Lori returned to the residential center, I no longer felt comfortable about the center's ability to handle her special needs. I was furious that they had considered placing her in a psychiatric ward without having a doctor examine her or even bothering to check on her behavior at school. I had spoken to her teachers, and although they had noted that her schoolwork was not as good as it had been previously, they had seen no negative behaviors. I no longer believed that the program staff possessed the necessary knowledge or the desire to work with Lori.

> *I no longer believed that the program*
> *staff possessed the necessary knowledge*
> *or the desire to work with Lori.*

A few months later I learned that Lori's residential program would be turned over to a person who had been working at the house for the past year. I knew that this person lacked skills and often disciplined the residents in inappropriate ways. Regimentation seemed more important than understanding the residents and treating them with love and compassion. Now I felt even more strongly that Lori should live somewhere else.

Once again we contacted the GGRC. This time they recommended a program in San José called Twelve Acres, which was operated by the Christian Science Church. We visited the combined school and residence, and they accepted Lori into their program. However, we had to find a practitioner for Lori, as physicians, psychiatrists, and psychologists were not part of the Christian Science program.

The Christian Science view of healing is based on the belief that the universe and man, as created by God, are perfect. The role of the practitioner is to put into practice God's law of harmony. Practitioners prayerfully work to destroy discord, disease, and other evidences of evil in order to bring lives into accord with God's law of love so healing can occur. Practitioner training involves deep, private study of the Bible and the writings of the founder and first practitioner of Christian Science, Mary Baker Eddy, particularly her book *Science and Health with Key to the Scriptures*. Practitioners must also take intensive courses on healing from an authorized teacher.

I asked several friends to help me choose a good practitioner, and I eventually found one who would see Lori as often as needed, usually once a month, but more often if necessary. The practitioner told me she would do her best to help Lori have a healthy attitude so that she could continue with whatever programs she was involved in.

The Christian Science program, of course, didn't allow

the use of medications. By now Lori had been off them for several months, so this wasn't a problem. I asked the staff how they handled children if a seizure occurred. When I saw the blank look on their faces, I described a seizure. They told me that some children had "episodes" and that when one occurred, they helped the child feel comfortable until he or she was again ready to participate in the activity taking place. The situation was handled where the episode occurred and without making a big deal about it. This kept the child from feeling strange, and the other children learned to accept the situation calmly. The result was that the child had fewer and fewer episodes. Since Lori had only one known seizure in her life and wasn't currently on any medication, the risk seemed minimal and worth taking.

For the next three years, Lori lived at the Christian Science home. She adored her house parent, a delightful middle-aged woman who showered her with warmth and love. Lori showed no signs of having an "episode," and she blossomed in self-assurance and skills. She came home once a month and on holidays. At those times, of course, our entire family was again consumed by her needs. But we seemed to have found the best solution possible for all of us, and I couldn't have been happier.

I was not, however, happy in my marriage. At the time Lori moved to Watsonville, I had a lot of unfinished business from childhood. Feelings of abandonment and shame made me feel guilty for Lori's condition and the impact it had on our family. Still, when Bill and I decided to have a third child, we considered our marriage healthy, despite the strain that Lori's special needs had placed on it over the years. That in itself was remarkable, as at the time any kind of problems children had tended to be attributed to a poor family environment, especially to poor mothering.

> *Feelings of abandonment and shame made me feel guilty for Lori's condition and the impact it had on our family.*

Fortunately, such theories were about to become a thing of the past, thanks in part to innovations that were pushing American society in new directions. The Human Potential Movement was just getting started, and many religious, psychological, and therapeutic trends were emerging and converging to challenge entrenched customs and conventional wisdom. As with many national trends, California was on the cutting edge of change.

Large Group Awareness Training (LGAT), Erhard Seminar Training (EST), Gestalt therapy, Transactional Analysis (TA), and Mind Dynamics were all new. These and similar concepts (most of which were soon labeled "New Age") may have shocked the conservative establishment, but many of them seemed to me potentially powerful ways to help establish healthier relationships by understanding myself and others better. At the heart of these innovations were group participation and support, things I had taken for granted as a child raised by an extended family. At an early age I had learned that, for better or worse, people grow and form identities through social contact, and I found this approach very congenial and conducive to personal growth.

While we were living in Albany, Bill and I had met regularly with three other couples from our church to discuss "Jesus' Teachings," a topic I had begun studying when I was twenty. This group was like an extended family, and on holidays we would have family get-togethers. The adults were like parents to all of the children. They were very loving and supportive, and I knew that any of them would care for my children as their own. Eventually we all moved to the suburbs, but we still got together for holidays and from time to time for Jesus' Teachings, which by then had been augmented by group awareness training techniques.

Our group focused on relationships and the role interpersonal communication played in self-esteem and in defining relationships with others. We practiced reading body language and tones of voice, something that was already ingrained in me. As the youngest child observing my precocious sister, Lou, and my hyperactive sister, Shirley, I had learned to be quiet and take my cues from the ways others expressed their moods. We also worked on developing trust and learning to speak the truth in love.

In 1970, a larger Jesus' Teachings group planned a week-long retreat at Eschelon near Big Sur, and Bill and I decided to attend. The retreat was much like the training workshops held at the nearby Esalen Institute in the late 1960s under the leadership of Fritz Perls, the founder of Gestalt therapy. One of Perls's most famous techniques was the "hot seat," in which a member of the group and the therapist worked one-on-one on a particular problem while the rest of the group remained silent. Afterward, the others gave feedback on how they were affected and what they observed.

This therapy often elicited very powerful, unresolved feelings, and Bill's experience on the hot seat brought to the surface raw emotions that were difficult for him to handle. At the end of the week, Bill and I were advised to not return to our small group until we had had private counseling for a while.

In the fall we began counseling sessions with Dr. Muriel James, soon to become internationally famous for her work in TA. Founded by Eric Berne, Transactional Analysis viewed people as basically "okay" and thus capable of change, growth, and healthy relationships. TA therapy focused on understanding the interaction between parent, adult, and child ego states and learning to communicate from the inner adult.

In counseling, both Bill and I became very emotional. Dr. James gave us tools to help us communicate, which to this day I find immensely helpful. In fact, I went on to study TA for eight years, applying it in my own family's dynamic and in my work. At the time, however, these tools did not remove the sadness I felt for placing Lori in a residential home or my anger with Bill and myself for agreeing to send her away.

Eventually, in a very straightforward manner, Dr. James told us that regardless of our sadness, at least one of us had to put aside our emotions and function as an adult. Her advice was characteristic of the assumptions of the Human Potential Movement, especially EST, which focused on getting in touch with yourself, seeing things as they really are, and learning to accept them and not blame others for where you find yourself in life.

> *Regardless of our sadness, at least one of us had to put aside our emotions and function as an adult.*

Given the historical context of our marriage, when the division of labor between husband and wife was much different than it is now, I had had all of the responsibility of caring for Lori. Bill, on the other hand, had been able to go off to work every day and not think about it. As difficult as that had been, it had forced me to work through some of my emotions.

Counseling provided me with more tools to do that. It helped me see that buying into shaming messages from the surrounding culture led only to feelings of sadness, guilt, and anxiety. I could choose not to swallow the message, or I could continue to feel ashamed by blaming myself. This required me to trust my judgment, even if it went against custom and authority. Becoming aware of what was really going on in any given situation, including my own feelings and desires, allowed me to make decisions based on what "was" instead of on what "should have been."

What I heard Dr. James telling me was that I needed to accept the situation, move on as an adult, and make the most of my life. I was now ready to do that, but even after a year of counseling, Bill's emotions were very unstable. He had never shared his feelings with me, perhaps because until the hot seat incident he had never been in touch with them himself. Now he was in constant emotional turmoil, and I found that I could not deal with the demands he placed on me.

> *The upheaval was so great that I felt*
> *I was hanging on to my sanity by a thread.*

I had never wanted to be like my mom, and I never would have taken a step toward divorce if I hadn't already tried every avenue open to me and done everything I knew to prevent it. But the upheaval was so great that I felt I was hanging on to my sanity by a thread. I was being consumed by Bill's emotional problems and felt that the life was being squeezed out of me. At last, communication broke down completely. I reached a point where I knew that if I stayed in the marriage, I would end up stuck in pain and trauma, when what I really wanted was to move on in life and grow.

In 1973, Bill and I divorced. With that decision, my family became what I had never wanted it to be—one of the 95 percent of families with a disabled child and an absent father. As painful as that was, I trusted I had done the right thing by choosing a life-giving path.

chapter six

The Burden
of Choice

I *believe* that options are always available in life and
that we are responsible for choosing among them. At
times our circumstances can be such that the options available
offer only a choice between the lesser of two evils, either of
which will have undesirable consequences. Still, we must
choose. Divorce had been a choice like that for me, and I
would soon have to make a choice like that for Lori.

Soon after Bill and I separated, I began to work full time. I had to. I continued to live in our five-bedroom house on a half-acre, and I just didn't have enough money to pay all the bills. I periodically received child-support payments, but the amounts were small and seldom on time. For several years, our neighbors' casseroles and good will helped sustain us. Keith and Lesli would joke about my passing the bone from one soup pot to the next, pretending we had meat. I don't think it was quite that bad, but I sure appreciated eating something besides soup!

In 1976, along with several other California parents who had a disabled child, I was asked to participate in a National Health, Education, and Welfare Department (NHEW) documentary film funded by the Sage Foundation. NHEW wanted to come into our home and film our everyday family living. The hope was that by focusing on the subject, other states might follow California's lead and develop regional systems that could better assist families by coordinating services for the developmentally disabled.

For two weeks, the movie crew taped interviews with Keith, Lesli, and me and photographed us eating, playing, and talking with Lori. When I agreed to participate, I had no idea how trying this experience would be. I was photographed laughing and crying about the struggles with Lori's situation, the breakup of my marriage, and my concerns about Keith and

Lesli. I had not known—could not have known—that raw emotions would resurface and sear me as I relived past experiences. After several weeks of flashbacks and tears, I returned to normal, my emotions spent.

My heart overflowed with gratitude for being part of an event that celebrated Lori's life.

The forty-five minute film *What Do We Do Now?* premiered in San Francisco. Lori attended, and she surprised me by standing tall and acting demure when the movie viewers complimented her. She sensed the key role she played in the movie and politely said, "Thank you," as she accepted their accolades. I felt truly blessed.

By now I had been dating for a while. I enjoyed the male companionship and a chance to be with adults. Being taken out to dinner was in itself a real treat. When I met Del through mutual friends, we began to date. Soon he proclaimed his love for me, and we talked about getting married.

Del was a very strong, gentle man who loved all my children. He quickly bonded with Keith and went out of his way to include him in every activity he could. He also cared a great deal about Lesli and was neither afraid of Lori nor mesmerized by her. She liked being with Del as well. We all enjoyed Lori when she came home from Twelve Acres, and when we went sailing or picnicking, she went, too.

Del was comfortable to be around, and I cared for him. Since my divorce, I had had to make all the decisions for my family by myself and carry the entire economic burden alone. Del loved us, and although he would bring no financial assets into the marriage, he had the potential to make good money. I thought that marriage would allow me to relax into our family, so I accepted Del's proposal. My family needed a father figure and was struggling to survive economically, so I felt it was the practical thing to do.

By this time, Lesli was eight years old and going into fourth grade, while Keith at sixteen had just graduated from high school and was attending a junior college on his savings and the money I could scrape up. Luckily, I had found a better job. I had been working as volunteer director for the juvenile hall auxiliary of the Contra Costa Probation Department. The position was funded as a nonprofit organization, which meant my salary was moderate at best. My new job was a full-time position as an intake worker at the GGRC. Life was looking quite a bit better.

Then, one week before Del and I were to be married, there came another blow. Lori's houseparent had retired, and Lori began acting out. Everyone at Twelve Acres knew that she was in agony over losing her beloved houseparent, but no one seemed to be able to help her adjust. When she was distraught, she would run off across a field near the residence to get the staff's attention. I received an urgent telephone call from the Christian Science residence telling me that I had to move Lori immediately.

Frantic once again, I spoke with the GGRC, for which I now worked, but nobody had the slightest idea what I should do. Fortunately, a young couple who knew Lori and had worked with her at Twelve Acres offered to let her live with them and their four-month-old baby until Del and I returned from our honeymoon.

Del and I were married in June 1976. While we were away on our honeymoon, Bill filed claim for his half of the equity on the house. I had placed the house on the market, and it had sold, but the buyers backed out at the last minute. This put me in a time bind, and I knew that as soon as I got home, I would have to sell the house quickly at a reduced price. Of course, Lori was also on our minds. When I telephoned the couple, they told me that Lori was quite the "mother's helper" and that all was well, so Del and I relaxed and enjoyed our honeymoon.

When we returned home, I moved Lori into a respite center for a few days while I attempted to find another residential program for her. She now functioned at the level of a five- to six-year-old. She had partial aphasia and no short-term memory, although she communicated well enough to let her needs be known. She could write several words, was habit trained, and easily followed two-step directions. But she was also still hyperactive, did not understand danger, and awakened several times each night. The idea of caring for her at home still pervaded my being, but every time I entertained the possibility, I panicked at the thought of having to respond to her needs twenty-four hours a day, seven days a week.

As much as I loved Lori, I knew I could not care for her alone. It took several people to meet her needs, and for her safety, she needed around-the-clock care by trained staff. Lori learned well in a structured setting, and I knew that she would stay on a residence's grounds if the staff kept her actively involved in tasks and activities. She ran only when she wanted attention.

> *As much as I loved Lori, I knew*
> *I could not care for her alone.*

With the help of the GGRC, I spent two weeks visiting residential programs and talking with their staffs, hoping to find a residence that would accept a brain-injured, active, retarded child who possessed very little impulse control. Sadly, not one of them would take such a child. The only alternative care—the absolute only one available at the time—was a state hospital.

Agnews State Hospital was located in Milpitas, near San José. Vast lawns and towering palms and citrus trees surrounded its Mediterranean Revival–style buildings, with their concrete walls and tile roofs. Agnews was well known for its beauty but also for the fact that its residents were hardly ever seen outside. I did not want Lori to be hidden away like that.

However, after the Lanterman Mental Retardation Services Act was passed in 1971, Agnews had begun to serve the developmentally disabled. The goal of the legislation was to build a comprehensive system in California to ensure that the mentally retarded would develop to the fullest extent of their capacity. In 1973 the act was expanded to include cerebral palsy, epilepsy, autism, and other neurological handicapping conditions resembling those of the mentally retarded.

Agnews actually had two separate campuses, one for the mentally ill and the other for the developmentally disabled. The latter had several large buildings that housed special programs geared to the severity of the patients' disabilities. The least restrictive program provided a workshop to which the patients could walk from their residences.

The fact that Lori qualified for admission to the workshop program was the deciding factor in my decision to commit her to Agnews, even though I knew that once I did, the state would have full authority. I did not want to put Lori in a state hospital, and I certainly did not want to give up my parental rights, but at the time, I felt it was the only viable alternative. With a heart full of sadness, I admitted Lori to the state hospital at Agnews.

Unable to see Lori for the first four weeks during her adjustment period to the new environment, I felt absolutely helpless. Though I knew I couldn't care for her at home, I didn't feel comfortable with my decision. I spent my days and nights missing her, wondering about her, and praying for her.

When I finally got to visit Lori, the change in her personality shocked me. She looked and acted lethargic, drooled, and had difficulty speaking. I asked the staff whether she was attending the workshop. I was told that she wasn't because she couldn't cope with leaving the unit. I wanted specifics.

Evidently one day she had played hide-and-seek among cars parked on the hospital grounds. Another day, she had climbed on a tractor and pretended to drive. These activities were typical of someone with the mental age of five, the grounds were well protected, and cars seldom moved around the campus. Nevertheless, the hospital considered her behavior unacceptable. There were no other suitable activities available, so Lori sat in her unit, drugged and in a stupor. She recognized me, but she couldn't lift her head because she was so heavily medicated.

> *Lori sat in her unit, drugged and in a stupor.*

Brokenhearted and angry, grieving for Lori and the situation, I left. When I got home, I called the regional center to ask for guidance. They told me that the only way I could influence Lori's care was to complain to individual members of the hospital staff, who changed every few hours. In other words, I had to raise a ruckus. They also suggested I contact the State Advocate's Office, which I did. That office appointed an advocate who would make several calls inquiring about Lori's health and what was happening with her, thus "red-flagging" Lori's chart so the staff would be more cautious about how they handled her.

When I next visited Lori, I found that the staff had moved her to a totally locked unit with residents who behaved like wild animals and scarcely seemed human. In the living area, the residents were situated around the room in various odd positions, rocking and making strange sounds. The furniture consisted of metal chairs bolted to the floor and a TV mounted high on a wall. Watching TV was the only activity available.

One minute some residents would be curled up in chairs; the next they would hurl themselves across the room. I kept a constant watch in case any of them launched themselves in my direction. The staff stayed in a windowed, locked cubicle in the middle of the room. To get the staff's attention, the residents had to bang on the window until someone finally opened the door.

I was shocked, and as I drove home, my heart ached. I had spoken to the staff and called Lori's advocate. What more could I do? Had I worked so hard to get Lori the education she needed to have her end up like this? If so, it would have been more compassionate to have locked her away in a hospital earlier instead of trying to teach her how to be part of the community. I couldn't accept that. I was so angry I wanted to rip the hospital apart.

I channeled my anger into talking with anyone and everyone who could possibly affect the conditions I had seen at Agnews. When I didn't get the results I wanted from these discussions, I flooded the place with visitors. If I couldn't help Lori, at least I could educate the public about how Agnews was using their tax dollars. By this time, Lori was known and loved in our little community of Alamo. To reveal the abhorrent treatment of patients at the state hospital, I made certain that as many articles as possible were submitted to the local newspapers, and I made a list of every important person I knew who would agree to visit Lori.

> *With every visit, my anger*
> *and frustration grew.*

With every visit, my anger and frustration grew. At one visit, I found Lori sitting in soiled clothes. Disgusted and angry, I immediately located the bathroom, only to find the door locked.

"Why is this door locked?" I asked the staff.

"For the residents' safety," came the reply.

I didn't scream at anyone, though I certainly wanted to. "This is ridiculous and inhumane," I said.

I pointed out that they sat locked inside their little cubicle while the residents were locked out of the bathroom. "Lori is habit trained but denied access to the bathroom. There is absolutely no excuse for her to live in this degrading manner."

"If Lori needs to use the bathroom, she must get our attention," one of the staff said.

"And just how do you expect an overmedicated disabled child to get your attention?" I asked.

The attendant stared at me as if I had dropped in from outer space and didn't speak her language.

Lori had no ability to deal with her situation, but I did. Patients had no access to their clothing, so I forced the staff to open the padlocked cupboard where Lori's clothes were stored. I took out soap and a washcloth so I could clean her up. Though aware of my presence, Lori was so zoned out that she didn't realize what was happening.

I kept up my questioning until I finally realized that the staff didn't care what I said and didn't plan to change. When I left, I called the State Advocate's Office again and lodged more complaints. I also contacted the director of the hospital, the regional center, my California representatives and senators, and the federal government, informing them about the inhumane treatment taking place in a program funded with tax dollars.

On one visit to Agnews, I asked about toys and games and was told that the residents would hurt themselves with them. Before Lori entered the hospital, she had enjoyed pre-reading, as well as working puzzles, sewing, and coloring. So I took her out and bought her crayons, coloring books, puzzles, and a guitar. I told the staff that Lori would not hurt herself or others with these things. Yet when Lori returned to her unit, the staff immediately took them away from her, and they were never seen again. When I learned about this, I was livid, but the only thing I could do was to bring toys Lori could use while she was out with me. I allowed her to take one toy back to the hospital, even though I knew the staff would confiscate it at the door. Lori soon learned that she could keep a toy until she entered.

On another visit, I noticed welts on Lori's wrists and ankles. When I asked about them, I got no response, so I began dropping by at irregular times to see her. One time I found her tied by her hands and ankles to a chair. I was told she had been in this position for three hours because the staff "didn't want her to hurt herself." The welts had resulted from Lori's attempts to escape her bonds.

On the next visit, Lori's clothes looked like rags. Although I brought her new clothes every month, they seemed to dissolve into thin air. On one occasion, I noticed a staff member wearing a T-shirt a family member had made and given to me for Lori. Even though I didn't have a say about what she wore at the hospital, I did change her before we went out, and she wore the change of clothes back to the unit. At least she could feel good while she was out.

Through all of this, Lori showed an uncanny ability to draw good people to her. Since she was not allowed outside, I suggested that the staff request a foster grandparent to train her by walking with her. Finally, the staff agreed and assigned her a Filipino gentleman. He walked with Lori at least once a week. Lori, of course, loved the walks and looked forward to her foster grandfather's visits, though he spoke little English.

"Aren't you afraid she might run away?" I asked him.

He smiled and said, "We just walk quickly, and then she does not think of running."

When I would ask Lori about her foster grandfather, she would smile from ear to ear and say, "We go walk."

This proved that with proper supervision and activity, Lori could be trusted outside the hospital, yet after six months the foster grandparent program ended, and Lori was once again locked inside.

By now I had toured all the state hospitals and had seen firsthand the bizarre behavior that accompanies deprivation. When patients don't receive adequate touching or other stimulation such as talking and appropriate activities to help them connect with the world, they often rock as a form of self-care. Starved for touch, some patients hit and bite themselves. Lori had never done these things before she was admitted to Agnews, I think because she had experienced love from the beginning and had developed a sense of self-worth.

Because of the way she was treated, now when Lori became upset, she would hit her head against the wall until she either made a big hole in it or knocked herself out. To gain attention, she would bite herself until she drew blood. She often mimicked those around her, and when staff reacted, she would repeat the behaviors.

> *By now I had toured all the state hospitals and had seen firsthand the bizarre behavior that accompanies deprivation.*

During the course of Lori's hospital stay, the regional center and I found and placed Lori in three different residential homes, hoping for a less restrictive environment. She lasted no more than five days in any of them. She ran away. She figured out when she wasn't being watched and used her ingenuity to disappear, most often in the middle of the night. But she actually loved being found and enjoyed the excitement of the rescue. The staff, however, couldn't handle the dangers inherent in her disappearance and the subsequent involvement of the police or a passing motorist. Everyone attempted to instill in her a fear of punishment or concern for her safety, but to no avail.

All people need to feel acknowledged, important, and loved. Lori had grown up having those needs met, and now that they were not, she picked up on the behaviors around her and took them to an extreme to get the attention she craved.

The hospital staff moved her several times, each time in order to deal with a more extreme behavior, but wherever they put her, she soon became top gun. In whatever section she was placed, she developed the most extreme behaviors of all the residents. I think her motto was "Whatever they can do, I can do better."

Since Lori had been on a patterning program as a child, she was very strong. She could hurl a chair across the room or throw a tantrum that would require three hefty adults to subdue her. At Agnews she learned the behaviors of a strong, wild animal, and when the staff or other patients pushed her, she unleashed those behaviors on them.

Anyone living in an institution develops behaviors to cope with the living conditions. Lori survived by grabbing any food in her sight and laying claim to anything in her vicinity. If things didn't go right for her, she destroyed whatever was around her. If there wasn't anything around her, she would destroy the clothes on her back. While I would never condone her behavior, I think it sprang from two things—her need for love and attention and her strong will to live, neither of which faltered during those dreadful years at Agnews.

After Lori had been in the state hospital for several months, she functioned at the level of an eighteen-month old and was closer to a wild animal than a human being. Her regression stunned me. I didn't know what more I could do to initiate changes in such a large institution. A seemingly impossible task loomed before me.

chapter seven

*Through
the Maze*

A s I *continued* to try to improve Lori's living
conditions, I felt I had entered a maze. I followed
path after path. Some of them looked so promising that I was
sure I was going to reach my goal, yet in every case I eventually
ran into a dead end.

❧

On one of the many occasions I spoke to the staff at the GGRC about Lori's institutional "care," they referred me to a legal advocate. After listening to my story and agreeing to take Lori's case pro bono, the attorney advised me that the only way I could win a lawsuit against the hospital was on the grounds that it was denying Lori an education.

The reason for this was that at least 40 percent of the funding for California state hospitals came from the federal government, which had mandated that all disabled children were entitled to a free education. Federal monies supported the education of developmentally disabled children until they were twenty-one. On those grounds, I filed suit against Agnews State Hospital.

The lawsuit took seventeen months. Several months went by before it was even filed. Finally, Agnews agreed to provide Lori and other developmentally disabled minors with an education. Although we had won the lawsuit, progress was slow. Agnews did clean out a small room and hire an aide. Ironically, she spoke only Spanish. Nevertheless, she was a very caring person, the kind Lori had always responded to, and I felt that at least Lori would be receiving good vibes until a more substantial program was developed. While I waited, I moved on in my attempts to help Lori, and eventually I lost track of the program.

About the same time that I initiated the suit against Agnews, I found out that there was going to be a family press conference in the rotunda of San Francisco City Hall. The focus was on conditions in state hospitals. I attended along with other families of the disabled. The press interviewed me, and I told them about Lori's plight. After the interview, the television crew went to the hospital. Since I had to return to work, Del and my mother accompanied them. Someone must have tipped off the hospital, because the grounds patrol met them at the gate and wouldn't let the crew in.

Del and my mother went in and brought Lori outside for a picnic, and the interview took place there on the grounds. The camera crew filmed Lori during her outing and while she ate lunch. She ate like an animal and appeared frightened that someone would take away her food. Nothing could have shown more clearly Lori's descent than this film, which stood in dramatic contrast to the one NHEW had made six months earlier, before Lori had lived at Agnews. That evening the television news exposed the conditions at the state hospital.

Alleluia!

> *Nothing could have shown more clearly Lori's descent.*

I felt good about my role in exposing Agnews' deplorable treatment of patients, and at first it looked as if things would change. The interior of Lori's residence was soon painted, Governor Jerry Brown made a special visit to the hospital, the state removed the director of the hospital and placed an interim director in charge, and I was appointed to the State Hospital Advisory Board. With the appointment, I thought I would be able to effect more changes.

Later, however, I came to see my appointment to the board as a joke. Ed Pye, who began the regional center system in Northern California, had once told me that if an agency has a squeaky wheel, all it has to do is to put it in the inner circle or give it an advocacy position. The wheel gains pride in the appointment, and then little by little becomes just like everyone else in the agency—a well-oiled piece of machinery touting the agency's line.

This wheel never got that far. During my two-year term on the Advisory Board, I was never once informed of a meeting, though I telephoned many times to ask when one would be held. The answer was always the same: Since changes were being made, no meeting had been scheduled. No one lied. Meetings simply weren't scheduled, and my appointment amounted to absolutely nothing.

In the end, there were no monumental changes in the system. The one that affected Lori most was that the staff now accompanied us whenever I visited her. In order to visit, I had to call ahead and make arrangements. If I just dropped by, usually no one answered the bell. When they did decide to let me in, they told me to wait outside. After several minutes, one or two of the staff would meet me and then stay with me the entire time I was with Lori. They stuck to me like glue until I left. The only time I was able to be alone with Lori was when we left the building.

❧

Friends and relatives were forever suggesting one more, just one more, possibility to help Lori. One idea originated with my mother-in-law. She told me that a faith healer would be in the Bay Area and urged me to attend one of the gatherings. She gave me a great deal of information about the faith healer. As she spoke, I flashed back to what I had learned in childhood about all the crippled and ill who were brought to Jesus for healing. I believed that miraculous healing could occur. After all, I had already experienced a spontaneous healing in my own life as the result of focused prayer. And I didn't believe that a person had to be in a particular spot at a particular time, touch the garment of a healer, or engage in specific rituals to be healed.

> *Did Lori have a specific role to play in life*
> *that I wasn't aware of?*

But I still had a lot of questions in my heart. What is healing? What would that look like for Lori? Most of the stories in the Bible portray healing as moving people toward physical "normalcy." But was there a reason my daughter was developmentally disabled? Did Lori have a specific role to play in life that I wasn't aware of? Despite my questions, I wanted to try anything that could possibly help her. I also loved my mother-in-law and wanted to honor her by doing what she suggested.

I asked a friend to accompany me to the healing service, and for several hours she and I waited, along with hundreds of other people, on the steps outside the San José Auditorium. As I stood in line, at first I wondered what in the world I was doing. But then as I listened to the conversations of the people around me, I felt their excitement. Their hope was contagious, and I found myself hoping for a miraculous cure for Lori. When the doors finally opened, we poured into the auditorium. I was glad I hadn't brought Lori, as there was no way she could have stood waiting in one place for so long. Surely the power to heal would reach her wherever she was.

When I sat down, I saw many crippled individuals being helped in, and my heart went out to them. One was a boy with severe cerebral palsy. His limbs were distorted, and he appeared paralyzed. He grunted occasionally but didn't speak, and his mother fed him during the service. Blind people shuffled in, led by caregivers. The deaf came, as did the crippled and those whose movements, noises, and appearances indicated that they were retarded. Some had hideous skin conditions and tumors. Somehow their disabilities seemed so much greater than Lori's.

The healing service began. As the faith healer spoke, people throughout the auditorium began to swoon. A number of people were on the stage, standing in a row next to one another. When the healer put the palm of her hand on the forehead of the first person, he passed out and fell on the next person, who in turn passed out and fell on the person beside him, and so on down the line. They looked like top-pling dominoes. *Am I witnessing mass hysteria?* I asked myself. This and many other questions floated through my mind. *Are any changes actually taking place? And if so, are they long-term changes?* There was no way for me to know. At the end, I was ready to dismiss the experience as just another dead-end road I'd gone down, although I did sense that some in the audience felt much better for having participated.

A few days later, I met someone who had attended the event and swore that his life had changed because of it. This raised more questions. *Why would one person be helped and not another? Do the individuals themselves need to desire the healing?* If so, no amount of desire or prayer on my part could ameliorate Lori's condition, for as far as I could tell, she had no thoughts on the matter. I do know that this event did not change Lori.

During this time, I continually tried to locate a residential pro-gram for Lori that would allow her to live in a community instead of an institution. Although several residences consid-ered taking her, as a teenager she had trouble handling her emotions. Her energy often seemed out of control, and she still ran away to get attention. She would be taken to a new residence for a trial visit, and within a few days—sometimes even hours—she would run away or act out in such ways that staff couldn't handle her.

Nevertheless, I kept trying to locate a loving and caring environment that could provide adequate adult supervision. One of the residences I investigated was run by Synanon, a group that had originally formed to help drug and alcohol abusers and then branched out. Synanon had residences in several locations, but the one I was considering was on a large parcel of land in Marshall. It was based on communal living, and Lori would be able to learn basic home skills, such as sweeping, dusting, polishing, and some cooking and baking. Several adults would be assigned to her in her small residence, and one would be with her at all times.

Three disabled young people and their parents had indicated to me that they were very pleased with the accommodations and treatment there. After much investigation and evaluation, I concluded that it was a far better environment than the state hospital, and I visited the leaders of the commune and went through their indoctrination. This was basically a group interview with me on the hot seat. In a grueling and intimidating session that lasted for several hours, the leadership grilled me about my intentions. Finally, they accepted me. When the state approved funding for Lori to live at the residence in Marshall, Lori and I made the three-hour drive.

After a long wait on the premises, however, the group told us that they couldn't accept Lori for another week or two. The members had approved her residency on paper only. I took she home until she could be readmitted to Agnews. I stayed home from my job as a counselor at the GGRC and enlisted the help of girlfriends to ensure Lori's safety. I didn't keep her at home very long because although I believed she could reverse the aggressive behaviors she had learned at Agnews, I didn't know how long it would take me to retrain her. Lori still needed twenty-four-hour care.

> *Although I was willing to try anything that promised to improve Lori's situation, nothing seemed to be working.*

I had been so sure that Lori would be placed in the nurturing environment at Marshall, and now I felt sad, disappointed, and angry. From Lori's perspective, she probably just made a long trip in the car, visited at home, and then returned to the state hospital. As much as I wanted her out of Agnews, the residence at Marshall never materialized for her. A few months later, I learned that Synanon's Marshall community had collapsed due to infighting. In hindsight, it was best that Lori didn't move there, but at the time I was devastated.

Although I was willing to try anything that promised to improve Lori's situation, nothing seemed to be working. Lori's problems were always present in my life. Even though I didn't want to know about every crisis, the hospital staff would telephone to describe incidents in detail. At least once a month, and sometimes more, I would receive a traumatic call. "Lori has run away. We can't find her. She's been missing for three hours. The police and staff are searching." Of course, my reactions affected the rest of the family, as I frantically called the staff back to see whether Lori had been found, what the situation was, and whether she was hurt.

Somehow, Lori made it through all the events, but descriptions of her bouncing off the top of cars and flying through the air tore me apart. By law, the hospital had to report any "incident" that damaged a person or object. No one ever called me to report a good or pleasant situation. This robbed me of any sense of peace, and after a while I didn't want to answer the telephone. My constant companions were a pain in my stomach and a huge ache in my heart.

Exhausted by the search process, I finally accepted that Lori's behavior required her to live in a locked setting, and I stopped trying to find a better place for her. I felt that I needed to let go of my search in order keep myself balanced and care for the rest of my family. Although the process was very slow and I went in bumps and starts, eventually I learned not to fret over Lori's living conditions. When her needs surfaced, I acted in a positive manner, and I never once stopped visiting her or encouraging our family to include her in special events.

Then, just as I had resigned myself to Lori's institutionalization, a seemingly miraculous series of events occurred. Agnews' educational program had finally kicked in, and I began to receive favorable reports from Lori's schoolteacher. When her teacher was subsequently transferred to the state hospital at Stockton, she informed both the staff and me that Lori belonged there, not at Agnews.

In a regular community setting, Lori would have attended classes for the trainable mentally retarded, which meant that her fellow students at Agnews functioned at a lower level than she did. The residents at Stockton functioned at a higher level, and Lori's teacher thought she would fit in better there. The residents also got to spend part of the day integrated into the surrounding community. I was delighted. I had always known that Lori had few behavioral problems when she was active and learning. When she was in an educational or workshop setting, the reports were always 95 percent positive.

When I visited Stockton, I could see that the treatment was far more humane than at Agnews, and the hospital agreed that Lori could attend its community school outside the facility. But when I contacted the GGRC to arrange for Lori's transfer, I was told that no mechanism existed for transferring a resident from one state hospital to another. Devastated and angry, I notified the Stockton staff of the problem and waited. And waited. About a month later, just when I'd given up hope that Lori would be transferred, I was told that she had been moved to Stockton and was enrolled in their school. She was doing fine.

Needless to say, I was thrilled about the change. Since the GGRC hadn't been able to make the transfer happen, I asked who was responsible for the change. It turned out that Lori's schoolteacher had arranged for her transfer and then proceeded to have her bused to Stockton, only without proper clearances. Subsequently, she was fired.

I was moved that this teacher would risk so much for Lori and sad that she had lost her job. I attempted to contact her to express my thanks. Although I was never able to reach her, I will forever be grateful to her. I hope she is aware of the great contribution she made to Lori's life by giving her a chance to live more normally. Within a year of her transfer to Stockton, Lori's behavior was such that she was considered ready for placement in a community residential home.

When I least expected a change, the state made an intense effort to develop a program that would allow developmentally disabled people to live in community. Lori was selected as one of the first residents to participate. The educational center for Alameda County was in Oakland, so that's where Lori would attend her last year of public schooling. However, she would be bused there every day from a residence in Hayward, which was considered more appropriate for her because the student-teacher ratio was better. There she would get more attention during her transition to community life.

After her regression at Agnews, Lori began making positive changes almost as soon as she moved into her new residence. Her outbursts decreased as her skills increased and she became more comfortable with her surroundings. The center informed me that Lori was the most skilled student there and that she thoroughly enjoyed learning. What a thrill for me to hear positive words about Lori! When she was ready to leave the center eighteen months later, the staff held a graduation for her. She wore a cap and gown and proudly accepted her certificate.

Periodically, Lori participated in the Special Olympics, running laps, skiing, and playing ball. One of my biggest thrills was to see her running toward the finish line rather than away from me. In skiing she won the gold medal for slalom and the silver medal for downhill. I believe her lack of fear definitely contributed to her winning the medals. John Denver presented the awards, and when Lori happened to fall right in front of him, he kindly helped her up. As proud as could be, she accepted the medals. Her photograph appeared on the front page of the *Tahoe News*, and our family was awed that Lori had won top honors.

Lori's next residence was in Concord, close to a specialized workshop where she could learn many additional skills. She got to garden, and eventually, with supervision, she cleaned service station bathrooms. She loved working and gained a great deal of self-respect from it. She also learned to deal better with her frustrations when she wanted to communicate but could not. In the eighteen months that Lori attended this workshop, she was not involved in any major incident stemming from misbehavior.

Then one day the staff called me about problems at Lori's home. More calls came, and I received a letter stating that the group homes were undergoing major staff changes and asking for patience during the transition. I had patience, but my daughter did not. She couldn't handle all the changes, and eventually the staff called to tell me that Lori had jumped from a second-story window and run away. The police had found her and brought her to the station. They could see that she had broken her ankle, but they couldn't take her for treatment until the residential staff reported her missing. Thirty minutes after Lori was brought to the police station, the staff called to report her missing. She was taken to the hospital to have her ankle set and then sent back to the residence.

I immediately went to see her and investigate. For three years, Lori had shown no signs of such behavior. I learned that prior to this incident Lori had been home for a week with a cold. When I asked Lori about her cold, she said over and over, "Don't lock door. Don't lock door." I believe the staff had locked her in her second-story room so they wouldn't have to be bothered with watching her while she was home during the day. She knew where the steps were and used them regularly. The window was also hard to open. So I couldn't imagine why she would choose to jump from a second-story window instead of using the stairs, unless she didn't have access to them.

As soon as I arrived back home, the staff telephoned to advise me that in order to stay at the residence, Lori had to be able to get around on her own with the leg cast. Taking Keith's wife, Jenny, with me, I visited Lori to see what might be done. Lori got around fine except for negotiating the stairs. Jenny took the project in hand and showed Lori how to go up and down on her fanny. With that problem solved, Jenny and I left. I thought everything was now okay.

Once Lori's leg healed, however, she still seemed determined to get the staff's attention. She sneaked out the door and ran directly into the street, which of course got a rise out of everybody who saw her. A car hit her and threw her several feet into the air. Police and an ambulance arrived. The hospital treated Lori for minor abrasions and kept her for observation. When they reported the incident to me, the staff told me that Lori could no longer reside at the home, so she stayed in the hospital while I searched high and low for another residence.

With the help of the GGRC, I learned that there would be an opening at a residential home within a month. Meanwhile, I would have to provide around-the-clock care for Lori. I didn't bring her home, as there she was dependent upon me for everything. She also constantly talked about living at home, and I felt that if I encouraged her in the least, she would do anything that would force me to keep her home. I didn't want to reward her for what she had just put everyone through.

My dear Aunt Ellen came to the rescue. She and my uncle lived on a large piece of property in Lafayette, where the entire family gathered and enjoyed many holidays. Aunt Ellen always invited Lori to these events. She had also been kind enough to hire Lori, along with her aide, to clean for her twice a month. Now she offered Lori a temporary place at her home if I provided the necessary supervision.

My cousin and my mother helped with the night shift, and

I took the day shift until I was able to hire Gina, a friend of Lesli's, to care for Lori every waking minute. Gina was terrific. She was very low-key and understanding. She didn't project negative feelings and walked with Lori whenever Lori wanted to. She worked with Lori until an opening became available at the new residential program several weeks later. To this day I have a warm feeling in my heart when I think of Gina.

When Lori moved to her new home, she struggled to adjust to the staff and surroundings. I thought her adjustment was coming along well, but after five months, the staff telephoned to say they could no longer handle her. Brokenhearted that Lori didn't seem able to cope with living in the community and discouraged by the need to search for yet another placement, I didn't know what to do. Now no program in the state would take her. Not only was she a potential runaway, but she was also plagued by episodes of violent behavior.

Not only had I not found my way through the maze, but now I was right back where I had started.

The GGRC informed me that my only option was to readmit her to the state hospital at Agnews. Not only had I not found my way through the maze, but now I was right back where I had started. The more suitable state hospitals had waiting lists, and none had room for her in the near future. When Lori returned to a locked unit at Agnews, I felt as though I had committed her to a living death.

chapter eight

A Living Death

W*hen Lori* was recommitted to Agnews, she was twenty-six years old and had been living in community for five years. During her first stay at the state hospital, I had done my best to try to protect her, and when I couldn't, I had called attention to the problems. But institutions are difficult to change, and when Lori returned to Agnews, I lost the majority of my influence. I could show concern, but I was powerless to influence the day-to-day events of her life.

❦

Tears well up in my eyes as I remember how Lori's joy and free spirit succumbed to the apathy and ignorance of her caretakers at what was now called Agnews Developmental Center. During the eighties, the term "state hospital" had been dropped to shape the public perception that the hospitals were no longer viewing the residents as "patients," but rather as individuals with special needs, abilities, and interests who needed progressive habilitating training. That may well have been the goal, but nothing had changed at Agnews. Staff members came and went, so they hardly knew Lori's name, much less her family and her interests, and by the time she had lived at Agnews for two more years, she had lost much of her ability to behave appropriately.

Tears well up in my eyes as I remember how Lori's joy and free spirit succumbed to the apathy and ignorance of her caretakers.

Periodically the staff would call me. Once it was to tell me that Lori refused to get out of bed to eat. She had never had trouble eating, so I found this hard to believe. When I visited, I found that she hadn't gotten out of bed to eat a meal for three weeks. She had lost forty-two pounds and looked gaunt, and her eyes were very black and vacant. Although she did get out of bed while I was there, she was a shell of her former self and appeared on the verge of dying.

I was shocked by what I saw, but the staff could give me no satisfactory reason for Lori's drastic change. Since she couldn't tell me either, I began visiting several times a week to take her out for lunch. This gave her an incentive to get up and eat. Eventually her frustration subsided, and she began going to meals at the hospital.

Lori's behavior was again extreme and volatile, so whenever an episode occurred, the staff put restraints on her and medicated her heavily—whatever they felt was "required." At one point, she was on nine different medications. I would often find her sitting at the table in a stupor, drooling. She always recognized me, but just barely. I tried to put a limit on her prescribed medications, but I exerted absolutely no influence on the institution.

Through thick and thin, Lori had remained a part of our family, although we mainly saw her on holidays. On one visit, she had pumped our player piano for two hours, singing the entire time. What a thrill it had been to see her so happy and contented! Now it took several people to handle her, and she could no longer participate in family functions. We as a family couldn't help her be a part of the community. My heart cried out at the tragedy of her existence.

One day the staff called me to inform me that Lori had been raped. I felt as if someone had hit me with a brick. I couldn't believe that something so horrible could have happened in what was supposed to be the most protective environment in the state. I wanted to rush to her side and hold her, but I realized that she probably wouldn't understand why I had come. Then I wanted to know her physical and emotional state and if she was being comforted. But when I asked how she was, all they would tell me was that she was "medically okay."

"What exactly does that mean?" I asked.

The staff then described what they had found. I didn't ask for further evidence. Evidently, Lori had a severe asthma attack shortly after the rape, and the staff told me that she was being treated.

"Who did it?" I asked. "A member of the staff? A resident?"

They told me that an investigation was underway.

Shortly before she was raped, Lori had been moved into a coed unit. When the staff called to inform me of the change, they asked me to provide Lori with a new bedspread, as they were encouraging all the patients to have their own bed covering. During the same call, almost in the same breath, they asked me to sign a paper giving them permission to give Lori birth control pills.

"Why?" I asked. "Do you expect the residents to visit each other's bedrooms?"

"No, of course not," the staff member said. "We simply want to be cautious, as some residents are sexually active."

Now isn't that just great! I thought. Even at the time, the staff's desire to make Lori's room look nice while they started her on birth control seemed ironic, to say the least.

Of course I went to see Lori and talk with her. She could tell me nothing, and her face had a blank look when I spoke of the incident. From what I could tell, she had blocked out the rape and either didn't know what I was saying or didn't know what to say. Subsequently I learned that she had become very touchy and upset during a physical examination. She was aware that I visited, however, and thrilled that I was there with her.

> *From what I could tell,*
> *she had blocked out the rape.*

I was furious with Agnews for allowing the rape to happen and angry with myself for not being able to protect her. This may not have been a logical response, but my emotions were very strong, and as I had done so many times in Lori's life, I again searched my soul to see if there was any way I could take care of her at home. Yet as desperately as I wanted her out of that place, I couldn't get around the fact that she needed a team of adults to care for her.

Another time, I found Lori suffering from bruised ribs and contusions. Of course, I again complained. Eventually I found out that a staff member had been accused of killing a resident in Lori's unit. Two other unexplained deaths occurred, and six residents were found to have broken ribs. After the district attorney investigated, the police arrested a man and placed him in custody.

The director of state hospitals called a meeting to discuss the problem of abuse, and I attended, but I found no solace there. When I spoke with other parents about the lack of protection for Lori, only one family expressed concern about their child's care. The rest were so grateful for any kind of help in dealing with their child that they couldn't allow themselves to view the state hospital as negligent. They feared that if they pointed out the hospital's inadequacies, their child would be sent home to live. Every time I complained, I was told that if I didn't like what went on, I could take Lori home. However, I well knew whose tax dollars supported the institution, and I refused to be intimidated by their threats.

Eventually the executive director and the medical director were removed, and Agnews was placed on notice to make major changes. Over the ensuing months, I saw no changes in Lori's unit, and one problem after another surfaced at Agnews. After a great deal of thought, I wrote an appeal to the director of the hospital, describing the daughter I once knew and requesting an evaluation of the "treatment" the hospital provided. As a result of my letter, I had many meetings with the hospital staff.

Lesli and I attended every one of the meetings in order to share our love for Lori and express our concerns so the staff might begin to see the young lady buried alive within Agnews' locked walls. Changes gradually began to take place. Staff members were taught how to relate to the residents, and Lori became lucid and fairly well adjusted to her situation. Progress seemed slow, but just the fact that change was occurring encouraged me.

> *Progress seemed slow, but just the fact*
> *that change was occurring encouraged me.*

I was also able to make a change that made life easier for Lori. The staff continually called her Karen, and whenever they did, she would just look confused and not respond. So I decided that it would be best to legally change her name to the one she preferred and was accustomed to. I filed the papers, and Lesli and I went through the lengthy process of changing Lori's name so that "Lori" would appear on all her medical records and the staff would call her by that name.

I was in constant contact with the state hospital, and they sent me scads of information and asked for my input. Due to the charges of major negligence, the hospital lost federal funding and accreditation. After this happened, I responded to Agnews' most recent program plan with the following letter, in which I attempted to make constructive comments about the hospital's administration:

I have just finished reading your lengthy Comprehensive Plan for Client Services, Fiscal Years 1992/1993 to 1993/1994.

You have obviously spent a great deal of time and effort working through each concern. Circumstances do not allow me to attend the meeting scheduled for public input, so I am taking this opportunity to share my concerns regarding your proposed program.

(1) Overall report

I was struck by the fact that the entire plan appears to be a detailed description of how various staff members will be hired, trained, monitored, and fired and a list of the appropriate actions to take under any given circumstance. This obviously comes as a response to the charge of negligence.

Describing processes is commendable, but I urge you to go one step further and formally state the major goal of the state hospital, which is to serve the needs of its developmentally disabled residents. Focusing on the hospital's mission statement will encourage the staff, parents, and community to direct their energies toward meeting the residents' needs and not just correcting "negligence" or meeting the criteria established by the federal government in order to qualify for funding.

(2) Aggressive behavior

In training staff to deal with a resident's behavior, it is critical that staff members look beyond the action and try to understand the reason for the aggression. A resident's action is a form of communication, even when it is inappropriate or dangerous to themselves or others. When residents resort to physical action, it is usually because they have not found another, more appropriate way to communicate. Although their behaviors might be very logical to the resident, the staff views them strictly as acts of violence.

Teaching residents how to communicate and rewarding them for communicating in appropriate ways is critical for the safety of both the residents and staff. Therefore, it behooves you to state that verbal and physical abuses are inappropriate ways to communicate with residents and that training will focus on teaching staff to reduce residents' frustrations by encouraging independent and appropriate ways of expressing themselves. One obvious way to do this is to reduce residents' pent-up energy by channeling it into various physical activities.

> *Even though residents at the state hospital need total, supervised care, they are human beings, a part of families, and a part of their communities.*

(3) Staff attitude

The attitude of staff has a major effect on how residents behave. Even though residents at the state hospital need total, supervised care, they are human beings, a part of families, and a part of their communities. As such, they deserve to experience life, participate in families and communities, and be responsible for their own actions to the greatest extent they can learn to do so. They deserve to live lives characterized by dignity and love. When these expectations are written into the guidelines of hospital and staff members understand and follow them, they will work with a confidence and care that will be reflected in the behavior of the residents.

I write this response to your report with love in my heart for my daughter, and for all the other residents who find themselves living at the state hospital.

In 1993, I received a letter stating that the hospital was in the process of placing all of its residents in the community. Within a year, the number of residents decreased from five thousand to two thousand. Of course, I agreed with that, as I had long ago concluded that large institutions are not conducive to normal living for anyone and that Agnews was a particularly bad example of the kind of care state hospitals afforded. Just as lilies need good soil in which to grow, so do the developmentally disabled. But for most of its residents, Agnews was toxic.

Every year we were learning more about training brain-injured people and providing a safe environment in a home setting, and I hoped with all my heart that a suitable home for Lori would soon become available. However, several years went by and nothing developed. As time passed, I became more and more resigned to the fact that Lori might never live in a community setting. However, I never stopped believing that she could and should be able to do so, and I continued to ask myself if I had done everything possible to help her.

> *I became more and more resigned to the fact that Lori might never live in a community setting.*

chapter nine

Growing Above and Below

When all my efforts to help Lori ended with her back at Agnews, I began to look upward and inward for the answers that had escaped me. As I did, I realized that the lilies grow above as well as below. Long before they bloom above ground, they send roots deep in the soil. There in the dark, God gives them what they need to grow. I had to let go of Lori and let God work out the purpose He had for her life. My responsibility was to develop the gifts He had given me. As I began to do that, I also began to meet the needs of developmentally disabled people in ways I would never have imagined possible.

By the time Lori returned to Agnews in 1987, I had spent almost a quarter of a century advocating for her. For years I had struggled to help her stay part of a community so she could have the quality of life she deserved. *And now this?* It all seemed for naught. To love my child yet be unable to help her enjoy a better life was excruciatingly painful, and I wanted to scream out to God, *Why is there such pain? Why? Why? Why? Is suffering the only way we can grow and bear fruit in life?* I had many questions, but no answers.

I remembered the story of Job in the Bible, although I confess that it wasn't one I liked. I had never wanted to read stories about pain and hardship except in fiction, where they were obviously not true. Job was a righteous man who lost everything he had—including his children—due to circumstances he knew nothing about, wasn't responsible for, and couldn't control. Even though he was devoted to God, God allowed him to suffer immensely. Job's story was far too close to home for me. Like Lori's circumstances, the book of Job was to me a dark book and difficult to understand.

To deal with my feelings of frustration, hopelessness, and sadness, I began to keep a journal and to pray in earnest to understand what was happening to Lori. At first I received no answers to my questions, although writing helped ease my pain. As I kept seeking answers, however, I entered a period of spiritual awakening in which I finally began to glimpse the purpose of pain and suffering.

> *I finally began to glimpse the purpose of pain and suffering.*

Like Job, I believed that good people would be spared pain and hardship, and like him, I cried out to God. We cry out to God when we are desperate for answers, but God answers when we are prepared to hear and understand. Often that is only when we are in a dark and difficult place. I needed a higher light than that of my own understanding to reveal to me the purpose of suffering, and when I had spent myself in crying out to God, He began to answer me in a still, small voice.

In retrospect, I see that I was planting roots deep in the dark soil. Although I was not conscious of it, with each loss, I took another baby step toward feeling healthy and whole. I knew that some families of the disabled never recover. Instead, they end up lodged in the trauma of painful events, suspended in space over a tragic abyss. Sooner or later, in one way or another, all of our lives look like Job's, and I didn't want to get stuck in the pain, unable to grow and experience the fullness of life. I began to view all the things that happened to Lori not necessarily as losses, but as opportunities to grow.

Stretching, learning, and dealing with difficult issues often cause us great suffering, but all of us must be willing to lean into the pain if we are to be fully alive and have depth of spirit. As I look at Job's suffering now, I see that he blazed a trail of courage and integrity for others to follow. I only hope that some of the fruits of suffering in my life can be as meaningful to others as Job's have been to the many readers of the Bible.

During this period of spiritual awakening, I consciously strove to redirect my feelings and energies so that Lori's situation no longer played such a large a role in my life. For many years, much of the rest of my life had been on hold, and I had felt I was merely putting in my time and taking up space. I didn't want to do that any longer. I wanted to discover, enjoy, and share all the gifts God had planted in me.

I began to make choices for my life separate from Lori's, and as I redirected my energies, I felt as if I were awakening from a deep sleep. Try as I might to help her, there were only two things I was truly able to do. The first was to attempt to understand and deal with my own responses to her circumstances, and the second was to try to help others in ways that I couldn't help her.

Redirecting energy into pursuing my education had always helped me keep my demons at bay, and in 1977, while I was working for the GGRC and struggling to get the proper care for Lori at Agnews, I had begun work on my master's degree in public administration at USC-Sacramento. The classes were held once a month over an extended weekend of four days, and although it took me two years to get my degree, my studies allowed me to gain perspective on Lori's situation, gave me a sense of accomplishment, and provided me with resources to help others.

In an effort to figure out ways to get the government to provide more appropriate services, I focused my term papers and presentations on the needs of the developmentally disabled. I was well aware of how difficult it was to make even the smallest changes in an entrenched institution like the state hospital system, but I felt that I could at least pursue the knowledge that would enable me to make informed decisions. It was a start.

Money, of course, was the root of the problem, and federal regulations largely controlled the flow of money to state service providers. My research helped me figure out where power resided and where the money came from to support it. Eventually I became quite knowledgeable about how to access both public and private funds.

Still, no amount of information would bring about change as long as most people didn't consider services for the disabled a high priority. That was pretty much the case in the late seventies, although the situation was beginning to change. Advocacy groups for the developmentally disabled were starting to put pressure on the "powers that be." Special interest groups were becoming vocal and therefore heard. Working with the disabled was becoming big business as universities and colleges encouraged students to become "experts" in the field.

> *No amount of information would bring about change as long as most people didn't consider services for the disabled a high priority.*

But though more and more people were trained to evaluate and diagnose, very few new services were actually developed. Instead, what I saw over the years was that many of the techniques we had pursued with Lori, such as patterning, were now regularly included in rehabilitation and speech therapy programs.

While I was working on my master's degree, Del and I moved to Lafayette, where he started a restaurant—an old-fashioned creamery/coffeehouse. By the time I finished my studies, I was working as director of development for a rehabilitation center in Pleasant Hill. My commute was not as long, my job had greater responsibility, and with my degree in hand, my salary jumped by $1200 a year. Back then, that was a big raise.

❧

In 1981, near the end of Lori's first stay at Agnews, I became the executive director of Eden Express in Hayward. In the late 1970s, two Bay Area mothers with mentally ill children had gotten together to transform a building into a full-service restaurant where disabled young people could receive on-the-job training. The families got permission from Kurt Vonnegut's son, Mark, to name the restaurant after *Eden Express,* the book he had written about his battle with schizophrenia. The eighty-two-seat restaurant opened its doors in October 1980.

Seven months later, I heard that Eden Express was looking for an executive director. I decided to look into it, even though I knew that the restaurant was not yet running. Instead of me taking hold of the project, it took hold of me. The more I thought about it, the more I realized that this was an opportunity to help the disabled gain the behavioral skills they needed to work independently in an industry where they were needed. So I took the job, and for the next nine years I channeled much of my energy into that endeavor.

In directing the vocational program at Eden Express, I reexamined assumptions about the role of transitions in the lives of disabled individuals. For the first twelve years of schooling, much of special education focused on analyzing students' problems and training them in the three *R*s. This generated an enormous amount of data about training techniques and projections for success. In secondary education, the focus was on transition. My question was "Transition to *what?*" I proposed that we change our training to focus on what I called "the missing link."

I believed that if the purpose of special education was to prepare disabled students to succeed in the world of work, educators needed to teach them what the world of work required of them. The schools had to provide a catalyst for success. They had to look outward to see what businesses needed and then help them find graduates prepared for the job market.

I saw the food service industry as just one of myriad job areas where disabled students could confidently transition into adulthood and become positive, participating community members. For this industry to run smoothly, every person undertakes a distinct job, but the unit runs as a team because each person realizes the importance of his or her job, as well as its relationship to the other jobs. I believed that when provided with adequate and proper transitional training, students could gain the skills they needed to function as team players in a food service position.

To accomplish this, we needed knowledgeable people to describe employee expectations, but most often our information stopped at description of job skills and didn't include explanations of the behavior and communication skills that disabled individuals needed to become effective, long-term employees. We also needed a real setting where they could experience these job skills and behaviors. For the disabled, training had to be concrete and experiential, with built-in rewards. Once they were on the job, transition support for them and the employer was absolutely essential.

For the disabled, training had to be concrete and experiential, with built-in rewards.

In the program I developed, the disabilities of the trainees included schizophrenia, manic depression, brain injury, deafness, autism, blindness, developmental disablement, cerebral palsy, epilepsy, and learning disablement. Some trainees had long-term workers compensation injuries. The lowest IQ (as measured by the Stanford-Binet test) was 50; the highest fell into the genius range. The majority had a combination of disabilities, or emotional problems coupled with other disabilities, and many of them took some form of medication. What all these people had in common was the need to learn appropriate work behaviors and marketable skills.

Entrance into the program wasn't based on diagnosis or IQ, but on practical measurements such as the ability to follow a three-step direction, an attention span of at least fifteen minutes, the capacity to travel independently to the work setting, and not having had a violent outburst in the previous six months. The training program consisted of three to six months of full-time participation before graduation and job placement.

During this time, Del and I divorced, and while I was single, I traveled around the country giving talks on the subject of training the developmentally disabled and training professionals to start similar programs. As my program became a national model, I was featured on national television several times and in sixteen different magazines, including *People*. I also signed a contract to develop a made-for-television movie to be directed by Tom Barad. Stevie

Phillips wrote the teleplay, Linda Lavin agreed to play me, and Paramount Pictures said they would provide about 50 percent of the monies. However, after three years I chose not to renew the contract because I didn't want to expose my children to public scrutiny, so the movie was never produced.

In 1987, when I was desperately trying to find a community residence so Lori would not have to return to Agnews, I had contacted everyone I knew and some people I didn't know. I was quite fortunate to reach Dr. E. Fuller Torrey, a noted research psychiatrist and one of the most knowledgeable professionals in the country. I had hoped Dr. Torrey could provide me with information about residential programs suitable for Lori, but while he empathized with me and encouraged me not to give up hope, he could recommend no place for Lori, either in California or anywhere else in the country. However, he did send me a manual based on a study he had done with Sidney Wolfe.

Published in 1986 by the Public Citizen Health Research Group and National Alliance for the Mentally Ill, the book was entitled *Care of the Seriously Mentally Ill: A Rating of State Programs.* The book rated facilities for the developmentally disabled across the U.S. and listed the states that were initiating new programs as well as those that lacked adequate services. California's state hospital system's rating was "poor, lacking adequate conditions and services." On a scale of 1 (the best) to 51 (the worst), it came in at 42. This confirmed what I already knew from personal experience, and after I read it I no longer felt alone.

In an updated edition of *Care of the Seriously Mentally Ill* in 1990, Eden Express was listed as one of the vocational rehabilitation programs that were making a difference in people's lives. Although our program had begun slowly, eventually thirty students were enrolled at all times, and by 1990, 750 disabled persons had participated. At least 90 percent were placed in jobs, and 82 percent retained their jobs for up to two years. I felt a huge satisfaction in helping the trainees gain skills and move into jobs, and I was thrilled to receive the Special Award for Public Service to People with Serious Mental Illness.

> *Eden Express was listed as one of the vocational rehabilitation programs that were making a difference in people's lives.*

The award, however, arrived at a time when I found myself living with an unresolved tension. As Lori's advocate, I had learned a great deal about how developmentally disabled people can live in community, and I had tested the waters as to what worked and what didn't. On the one hand, I had created a successful training program based on a treatment style that worked for the disabled. On the other hand, my disabled daughter, whom I dearly loved, was still unable to participate in community.

I retired as executive director of Eden Express in early 1990, two weeks before I remarried. With my marriage to Gregg, I felt the boundaries of my life expand and my spirit blossom as I released the creativity stored within and channeled it in new directions.

Gregg and I both loved dancing. While I was growing up, dancing and drinking were two things Grandpa Alva wouldn't allow. He believed that dancing led to promiscuity and that if you took one drink, you would become an alcoholic. Since my mother had met Ted at a dance, Grandpa may have had a point about both of these activities. But although I didn't drink, I craved dancing. I felt I had music inside I simply couldn't contain.

I'm certain that my love of music was a gift from my father, and when I was young, that's how I filled my yearning for him. I could sit in church for hours listening to the choir sing. Being part of a choir myself has always made me feel like part of a family. When I'm singing, I feel that my heart is open and that I am sharing my emotions with an extended family of caring, supportive people. I have never wanted to sing solo.

Sewing was another creative outlet for me. My grandmother loved creating things and could sew anything from scratch. My sewing lessons began when I was four, and in the early years of my marriage to Bill, I sewed professionally to help pay the bills while he finished his college degree. When I felt lonely for Lori, I would create special outfits for her while I thought about all the beauty she had brought into my life.

Gardening was another connection to my past and to the loving grandparents who had nurtured me when I was young. I found working in the soil both life giving and life renewing, and I still loved watching flowers grow. One of my childhood memories is of sitting in church on a very hard pew gazing at the gorgeous stained glass windows. I began to work with stained glass in an adult education class in the late 1970s. Not surprisingly, one of my favorite things was creating glass scenes of flowers.

Gregg introduced me to the joy of creating with ceramics and encouraged me to express myself through painting as well. All of my creative interests eventually coalesced in a custom art business, Barbara's Touch, which allows me to continually experience the healing and joy of the creative process.

In 1993, Gregg and I decided to move to Bend, Oregon. I knew I had done everything possible to help Lori, but the feeling that I might be abandoning her still plagued me.

One evening before I went to sleep, I prayed about the question burning inside me: *Why does my heart still ache at the thought of leaving Lori?* Early the next morning I was awakened by the beautiful sound of birds singing. I thought at first I was still sleeping, but then I realized I wasn't. I wondered why I had never heard the birds sing in the morning before.

There are many things that go on that you are not aware of, said a still, small voice inside me.

"What does that mean?" I asked.

There are many beautiful things going on in Lori's life that you are unaware of.

I had a wonderful feeling of peace and comfort. However, by the time I was ready to get up, I had begun to doubt what I had heard and thought I had probably imagined it to assuage my guilty conscience.

The next night I asked specifically: *Is there more that I should do for Lori?*

This time the answer boomed out: *You will know when there is something to be done. Then you will be able to act.*

Wow! There was no way I could mistake the answer. I also felt a warm comforting feeling of being held in safe hands and totally protected from anxiety and worry. Knowledge cannot flow into a heart that is closed, and pain had cracked mine open. I was certain that the information was right, and I felt secure.

> *Knowledge cannot flow into a heart that is closed, and pain had cracked mine open.*

As soon as Gregg and I got settled in our new home, we made arrangements for Lori to fly up to see our place so she could have a visual picture of where we lived. While the trip was exhausting for Lesli, who accompanied her, it was a thrilling adventure for Lori.

I also visited Lori at Agnews as often as possible, and on one memorable visit I heard that she had a special male friend in a nearby unit. After an outing, I told her that I would love to meet him. She looked pleased, so I asked the staff if I could meet the young man. I was taken aback when I saw him. He was very short, had very dark skin and no teeth, and wore a helmet. I gasped. Obviously, I had some expectations that I didn't even know I had.

I introduced myself, and he acknowledged me briefly before taking Lori's hands very lovingly in his own. I asked them if they would like to sit in the dining hall for a few minutes. I didn't need to suggest it twice. They immediately went into the big vacant hall. He pulled out the chair for her, and she coyly sat down opposite him. They didn't say anything; they just held each other's hands and enjoyed being together.

My heart melted. Many nights when I had lain awake, listening, I could hear Lori's call. *Who will listen to her?* I had asked myself. *Who will know what is in her heart?* Already locked in her partially functioning mind and body, Lori was behind locked doors as well, seemingly doomed to a life empty of the joys of family and community. Yet, here she was—experiencing life and love—and I rejoiced that she was being heard. If this young man could bring my daughter happiness, how could I not love him?

I had assumed that life at Agnews had been nothing but a living death for Lori. But I was wrong. There were indeed many beautiful things going on in Lori's life that I was unaware of. Lori's life was very different from mine, but I had much to learn from her.

chapter ten

A Teacher
and a Guide

When I was no longer drowning in my own sorrow and viewing my circumstances through a veil of tears, I found that I no longer wept for Lori. I began to see that I had grown in ways I might never have if Lori had not been part of my life. I believe the same is true for everyone in my family. In many ways, Lori has been our teacher and our guide. We have learned a great deal more about ourselves and become stronger, better people because of her.

Until she was eight years old, Lori lived at home, and I did all I knew how to do to provide a loving, comforting family environment for her to grow up in, despite the fact that she had very special needs. After she was placed in a residential home, and later in the state hospital, her time at home was limited, but for many years her overriding desire was to spend time with her family. She rarely wanted to leave wherever we were present. We continued to include her in holiday events whenever we could, even though those occasions were usually marred by her hyperactivity, insomnia, and poor impulse control, which affected everyone present and whatever we decided to do.

On the one hand, including her in family activities gave Lori the freedom to express herself, and on many, many occasions, she literally beamed with happiness. Until she lived in the state hospital, never—not once—was she mean or vicious. She was gentle and loving with children and pets. On the other hand, the adult in charge had to be constantly alert and expend a huge amount of physical, emotional, and mental energy to ensure her safety. For the first eight years of Lori's life, I was the adult in charge, which meant that Keith and Lesli received less of my time, attention, and energy. I often wondered how they felt about growing up with a brain-injured sister, and not long ago I asked them.

Keith said that Lori was just his sister and that he didn't think about how she affected his friends or what he chose to do. He did bear the brunt of some of Lori's tantrums, however, and I know that he suffered when an older cousin once told him not to bring Lori's problems around his house. I think of Keith as a rock of affection and competence. As a child, he was always sensitive and caring, and I could depend on him to keep Lori safe. I have never seen him express anger toward Lori or be mean to her. He always tried to teach her and help her improve her skills.

> *Because of circumstances none of us could control, Lesli was normal and Lori was not.*

Lesli was a stunningly beautiful baby. When she was young, she looked just like Lori—a constant reminder to all of us that because of circumstances none of us could control, Lesli was normal and Lori was not. Lesli admitted that she had often wished she had a normal sister to "pave the way for her," but that whenever she thought of not having Lori as a sister, she realized that if Lori hadn't had a problem, she herself might never have been born.

Lesli said that she didn't remember anything bad about growing up with a retarded sister. She said that although she had vivid memories of Lori's tantrums, which frightened her, it has been more difficult for her to deal with Lori as an adult. After I moved out of state, Keith and his family followed, leaving Lesli and her father to be the ones Lori visits during holidays and the ones contacted when there's a problem. Lesli understands what Lori says, has great patience, and helps plan projects for her.

One thing Lesli remembers is that she hated to hear other kids use the word *retard* to describe anyone. Although I didn't realize it at the time, living with a disabled sister obviously made Lesli and Keith supersensitive to having problems "out of the norm." When Lesli was little, she had to get speech therapy for minor tongue thrust. Even though it was for a very short time, she told me later that she had felt marred by the experience. She was certain she had a handicap because she had to go to therapy. Keith told me he had felt the same way when he had to do a special eye exercise to enhance his reading. He, too, said he was very upset about the therapy because to him it meant that he must have had a handicap.

When Keith and Lesli moved away to attend college and Lori came home to visit, she felt very lonely. I explained that her brother and sister were at school, but she would wander listlessly through the house looking for them. She spoke about Keith with her voice full of sadness and sought reassurance that Lesli would be back, too, and that she would see her brother and sister again. Although adjusting to these changes was difficult for her, she eventually accepted the situation.

Bill is still very much a part of Lori's life. I recall one time when he took Lori out to lunch. She returned with a huge smile on her face and told me, "Go by self. Eat lunch. Dad." I hugged her, knowing how thrilled she felt with the special time she shared with her dad. She was one happy lady.

As for me, I thank God for Lori. No, my life has not been easy. But I do not beat myself up for the things I could not or cannot change. I enjoy life and all it has brought me, including its challenges. I feel that because of Lori, I have learned more than I would have otherwise about myself, the nature of life and mankind, and what it means to love unconditionally. Lori never fails to make me feel that I have been handed a gift of joy just by being in her life.

> *Lori has been a teacher and a guide for*
> *society as a whole as well as for her family,*
> *and she has been heard.*

When I was unable to help Lori in ways I would have liked, I channeled my energy into learning. As a result, I enjoyed a tremendous educational experience during which I earned a BA in social psychology, an MA in public administration, and an MA in holistic studies with an art focus. My education, in turn, has enabled me to make valuable contributions to the community at large, as well as to my own smaller, family community. In this sense, Lori has been a teacher and a guide for society as a whole as well as for her family, and she has been heard. Today the disabled are seen very, very differently than they were while she was growing up.

When Lori was young, many "experts" believed that mental and emotional troubles were primarily the result of poor parenting, especially by mothers. Few things seem as cruel as telling the mother of a mentally disabled child that the problem is her fault. Faced with the daunting challenge of caring for such a child, it takes a strong sense of self not to buy into the wrongheaded assumptions that support the institutions that make things worse instead of better for the mentally disabled and their families.

Mercifully, experts now agree that such theories, which have added immeasurable guilt to the already heavy burdens of parents of mentally disabled children, have little evidence to back them up. Most brain disorders are now seen as brain chemistry problems, not mothering problems; and with improved technology, infection has emerged as a prime suspect. Today, scientists recognize that the bacteria and viruses that frequently invade our bodies can trigger a host of major organic brain disorders.

The introduction of computed tomography (CAT) scans in the early 1970s was a great leap forward in diagnosis. Before then, only an X-ray could reveal damage to the brain, and then only in its most obvious form. CAT scans show subtle changes that can be tracked over time, giving researchers a more accurate sense of a microbe's impact. Magnetic resonance imaging (MRI), developed in the early 1980s, provides three-dimensional pictures of the brain, and positron emission tomography (PET) scans, invented soon after, have added motion. Now the bacteria and viruses that cause diseases like the flu encephalitis that damaged Lori's brain can be caught in the act.

> *Even with all the technological advances,*
> *there are still serious challenges for families*
> *of mentally disabled children.*

Knowing that many mental disabilities begin with a microbe, not a suffocating mother or a remote father, has removed the shaming and blaming from treatment. If technology and societal attitudes had been different when Lori was a child, I most likely would have known sooner what her problem was, and there would have been more medically appropriate ways to deal with it. Certainly I would have suffered less guilt. Yet even with all the technological advances, there are still serious challenges for families of mentally disabled children, for to a great extent, societal attitudes and institutions are slow to respond to their needs.

I honestly do not know specifically what I would do differently if I were faced with the same problem today. I still firmly believe that the disabled should be part of the family and included as much as possible in family activities. Today, however, I would definitely be more conscious of the impact that living with a severely disabled person has on the entire family. I would encourage every family member to grow from the experience, rather than just attempting to cope with the residue of the loss. Had I received better guidance and more understanding from professionals, I would have been a healthier person with more time and greater energy to invest in other family members.

If I were handed a child like Lori today, I would also live my life knowing that while we are all connected, each of us is a separate individual and that none of us can live for another person. To fulfill our distinct purposes in life, we must each use our unique gifts to the fullest extent possible. Lori makes her own contribution, as do I. Each of us gives whatever our circumstances and creative spirit allow. Lori travels her own road. Sometimes the way is rough, and she stumbles and falls; other times the path is smooth and she walks along without problems. The same is true for me.

No person's physical or emotional needs should consume another person. Sharing in and helping with someone else's load is different than taking complete responsibility for the life of that person. When one person in a relationship is as severely challenged as Lori, it's not only impossible to do that, but also destructive to both people in the long run. No person should require the total dedication of any other individual, and the reality is that the disabled need the dedication of more than one person to thrive, and even to survive.

I strongly believe that the disabled have the same rights as those without disabilities—no more and no less. Yes, they lack equal abilities, their basic needs are greater, and they require lots of assistance. Just like the lilies grow in clumps, needing each other in order to grow, the developmentally disabled need to be members of an extended, caring family— a community—in which an individual's choice to spend time caring for another is made as an act of conscious love where the gift of life is shared between the two. Love, time, and money are far better utilized when the disabled live in communities where we all share our talents and knowledge with them.

> *Love, time, and money are far better utilized when the disabled live in communities where we all share our talents and knowledge with them.*

We must also expect the disabled to participate in caring for themselves and contributing to their communities. Whether they sweep, carry items from one place to another, or prepare food, they need to participate in the daily chores that must be carried out. Lori knows the difference between make-work and meaningful work. She needs to be expected to accomplish real, daily tasks, and just like all of us, she needs the rewards that come from being productive.

Lori was born at a time when society was just beginning to learn about the differences in disabilities and how to train the mentally disabled. If she were born today, her chances of receiving an education within the community would be very high. I hope that community programs will continue to aid families and teachers in dealing with partially aphasic people and those with poor impulse control. Attending churches, shopping for food and clothing, riding buses, and visiting libraries are activities most of us take for granted. For the disabled, these are special events. We must encourage our community organizations to reach out to the disabled so that they might be included in those activities in ways that do not disrupt others.

I also hope that we will develop knowledge that will assist disabled people to maintain themselves in normal community living as much as possible without accruing excessive costs. When the State of California began phasing out Agnews Developmental Center, the cost of maintaining one patient was $250,000 per year. It is true that the cost of supporting a disabled person is far more than supporting a "normal" individual, but it should not be five or ten times as great. The fact is that the cost is so high because our society has developed an enormous number of professionals who make their livings from studying, analyzing, and developing plans for the disabled. In practice, however, all the money spent on professionals and their programs has not translated into services that meet the needs of the disabled or their families.

We have traveled a long way in hiring the disabled over the past twenty years. Corporations such as Home Depot, Costco, Safeway, and Target, to name a few, have come forward and hired the disabled. Today, the disabled work as customer reps, in volunteer organizations, and on computers. The list goes on and on, and I am proud to have been part of initiating this phenomenon, which was unheard of when Lori was old enough to be hired. Yet the time has arrived to make another shift. The educational emphasis now must be on developing additional special resources in our communities and including the disabled individual in our communities' regular functions. Institutionalization should never again be an option, much less the only alternative.

> *Institutionalization should never again be an option, much less the only alternative.*

My experiences with Lori over the years have taught me that there may be no simple answers for a family with a developmentally disabled child, but there *are* answers, and a family finds them as life unfolds one day at a time. Life is never static, and the answers that work one day might not work the next, just as the questions themselves change over time and from place to place.

Nevertheless, there is one principle that always applies: Whatever my particular circumstances, it is my choice how I respond to them. I don't always have the answers, and I can't always make things better, but I can look at the love and care that surrounds us all and respond to the continuous call to share with others that which I do have. Together, we can work toward understanding life and living our lives to the fullest while helping the disabled to live their lives to the fullest as well.

How They Grow

In 1997, a sequence of unusual events took place. Gregg and I were traveling in Turkey, and during a tour of the Blue Mosque, our guide told us about the wishing stones that Muslims use to request help from Allah. She showed us how to touch the stone in a special way while making a wish. I was the only one who wanted to try the procedure. There were two wishing stones in the area, so I followed our leader's instructions on each one. I didn't tell anyone what my wish was, but it was the same one that had been in my heart for years: I

wished that Lori could live in community. I made the wish
and then didn't think about it again while we were on our trip.

After we got home, I picked up our mail and started listening to the messages on the answering machine. There was
one from the East Bay Regional Center, and of course I
thought that Lori probably had a problem and that they were
calling to notify me. I returned their call, and to my complete
surprise, I was told that a new community program had been
developed with staff specially trained to help state hospital
residents adjust to community living. By now Lori had been
back in the state hospital for nine years, so the news came
as a great shock. I immediately remembered the wish I had
made at the Blue Mosque in Turkey.

God moves in mysterious ways, I thought.

Within two months of the phone call, Lori moved into a
group home in Hayward with two other disabled adults—
including her special friend from the state hospital—and was
able to attend various day programs in the East Bay. When she
first moved into this home, she suffered from severe asthma,
but after a year, it was no longer a major problem. The inter-
esting thing about Lori's asthma was that she would get it
when she walked. It was as if her system prevented her from
running away from the home while she settled in and
adjusted. If she couldn't control her impulse to run, an asthma
attack could control it for her.

One thing I know about Lori's life is that it's never dull.
While living at the group home, she has made several trips to

the hospital due to one problem or another. Once some food apparently got stuck in her windpipe. The only thing the staff knew was that she was having trouble breathing. After several visits to the doctor and a trip to the hospital for various tests, the doctor decided that Lori had a tumor, and I was asked to give permission for cancer treatment. I proceeded to visit, gather facts, and observe what was going on. Finally, I let the doctor know that I didn't think Lori had cancer. He had X-rays taken, whereupon they discovered the real culprit.

All of this took more than a month, and the only real damage done was that the special attention Lori had received gave her the desire to have more. Once home, she did her best to force the staff to return her to the hospital via ambulance, police car, or fire truck. She caused such a stir that the community services came together and requested that she not reside there.

Nevertheless, Lori continues to live in community. Currently she resides in a lovely home in Rodeo. The humorous part is that Lori signed her own lease. I asked if someone had cosigned, as Lori would have no way of knowing what she was signing. I certainly wouldn't want to have someone functioning at the level of a three- to five-year-old sign a lease on my house. The incident, however, is typical of the services in California.

Recently, conditions at Lori's house became questionable, and the Adult Protective Services stepped in to monitor the situation. The home was sold to another corporation, and the staff changed. The new staff members are conscientious and loving, food is adequate, and staff training is taking place, so the situation is much improved. Lori attends a day program and lives with one young woman. The two of them live independently with the help of a rotating staff that assists with food preparation, cleaning, washing of clothes, grooming, and outings.

Throughout the years that Lori has lived in community, she has had numerous outbursts, which I attribute to the fact that she has had to unlearn the extreme behaviors she learned in order to survive in the state hospital, where the loudest and most volatile behaviors received attention. Unfortunately, Lori now deals with the enormous task of trying to shed institutional behavior. This would not have been necessary if she had been maintained in the community. Although it is very difficult to modify her behavior, little by little the staff members are helping her learn appropriate ways to express her emotions.

With regard to her health, Lori's weight has climbed from 132 to 250 pounds, and she can no longer participate in the activities she once loved. She cannot ski or sail or ride a horse. Indeed, it is difficult for her just to walk. Her eyesight is marginal, she has high blood pressure, and two years ago all of her teeth were pulled because her gums were infected. Due to shrinkage and poor posture, she is now only five feet one inch instead of her original five feet four inches. She no longer sews or finds coloring a pleasure. Her main enjoyment now is watching videos or listening to music, although she still enjoys putting together a hundred-piece puzzle. The daily tasks of dressing, eating, and going to the day program are about as much as she can handle.

Still, since that miraculous phone call in 1997, Lori has lived in community. In her mid-forties, she could live for many more years. Her life is far from over, and no one knows what tomorrow might bring. However, her constant attachment to me is over. She loves visits with her family, but she also enjoys her own world. She freely states that she loves her home. Throughout her life, this has been my constant hope for her. I am thankful that she now lives in community, and I pray that she can continue to do so until her life on earth is over.

❧

As I look back over Lori's life and think about how the lilies grow, four things stand out in my mind:

They grow when they are in good soil tended by caregivers who love them as their own.

They grow when their families are themselves nourished and growing.

They grow when they learn life skills, do meaningful work, and have their own place in the world.

But most of all, they grow under the watchful eye of a loving God who knows their potential, sees their needs, and provides for them in His own time and His own way.

Acknowledgments

I thank my children, Keith and Lesli, for the pleasure they gave me and the patience they developed growing up in a complex family unit. They grew up to be beautiful, caring adults who continue to bring me joy. Most of all, I thank Lori for opening my eyes to the depths and complexities of life.

I also wish to acknowledge the many friends and professionals who encouraged me to record my journey so others might know that, although it may be difficult to see at times, there is a path.

I particularly thank Judith St. Pierre for her understanding and for her questions, which helped me examine my feelings about what took place along the way.

*B*arbara Munster received a BA in Social Psychology from California State University at Hayward in 1964, an MPA from the University of Southern California at Sacramento in 1979, and an MA from John Kennedy University in 1993.

Barbara's awards include:

- National Recognition for Service to People with Mental Illness, 1990.
- San Francisco Foundation's John R. May award for outstanding contribution to the Bay Area, 1990.
- Acknowledgment in the House of Representatives' Congressional Record, 1989 and 1990.

- Acknowledgment in State of California Assembly Resolution, 1973 and 1990.
- National Restaurant Association Award for Outstanding Training Program for the Disabled, 1989.
- Alumnus of the Year Award, California State University at Hayward, 1988.
- Acknowledgment in Alameda County Board of Resolution, 1990.
- City of Hayward Recognition Award, 1990.

Now retired, Barbara spends much of her time in her studio painting and working with various forms of glass. She also does volunteer work at the local Volunteers in Medicine clinic, and after two years of intensive work and one year of internship, she has recently completed the requirements for becoming a spiritual director.

In addition to her three children, the lilies in Barbara's field now include four grandchildren.